San Diego Christian College
2100 Greenfield Drive
El Cajon, CA 92019

WHITE'S RULES

SAVING OUR YOUTH
ONE KID AT A TIME

17.46

WHITE'S RULES

SAVING OUR YOUTH ONE KID AT A TIME

Paul D. White with Ron Arias

MORGAN ROAD BOOKS
NEW YORK

 MORGAN ROAD BOOKS

Copyright © 2007 by Paul D. White and Ron Arias

Published in the United States by Morgan Road Books, an imprint
of The Doubleday Broadway Publishing Group, a division of
Random House, Inc., New York.
www.morganroadbooks.com

MORGAN ROAD BOOKS and the M colophon are trademarks of
Random House, Inc.

Book design by Michael Collica

Library of Congress Cataloging-in-Publication Data
White, Paul D.
    White's rules : saving our youth one kid at a time / Paul D.
White with Ron Arias.
    p. cm.
    1. Youth with social disabilities—Education—California.
2. Problem youth—Education—California. 3. School
improvement programs—California. 4. West Valley Leadership
Academy (Canoga Park, Calif.) I. Arias, Ron, 1941– II. Title.

LC4802.5.C2W48 2006
371.93—DC22

                                              2006046732

ISBN: 978-0-7679-2419-1

PRINTED IN THE UNITED STATES OF AMERICA

10 9 8 7 6 5 4 3 2 1

First Edition

Except for the chapter 11 testimonials of Anthony de la Torre, Andrew Heiger, and Ellen Nims, as well as the passages about the Auschwitz survivor Eva Brown, I have changed the names of all those whose stories appear in *White's Rules* in order to protect their privacy. To further shield identities, I have tempered some details about several other people portrayed in the book. In all other respects, my students and their struggles, failures, and triumphs are real and true, as is my experience as their teacher.

To Valerie: X + 1

CONTENTS

ACKNOWLEDGMENTS

Thank you, Valerie Espinoza White, for loving me. If I've become a good man, it's because of you, sweetheart.

Thank you, Al and Elizabeth White, for the home and love and example you gave me. I'm sorry I waited so long to tell you.

Thank you, Anne and Pat Templeton. Even I would have given up on me, and you never did.

Thank you, Ellen Nims. I'm a teacher because of you, and the example and support you gave me.

Thank you, Scott Street and Ingrid Ylisto. You showed me that great teaching and personal integrity are inseparable.

Thank you, Russ and Judy Cleveland. Words can't describe what I owe you.

Thank you, Chuck Mills and Lonnie Lardner, of Hope's Nest, for your generosity in support of West Valley Leadership Academy and its activities.

Thank you, Ron Arias. Why you took an interest in my story, God only knows, but I'll always be grateful, and I'm honored to be your friend.

Thank you, Joan Arias, for your help with format and tone suggestions.

Thank you, Reid Boates, my literary agent, and Marc Haeringer, my editor at Morgan Road Books/Random House, for seeing the book through the long publishing process.

Thank you to Morgan Road Vice President and Publisher Amy Hertz. You started out publishing the West Valley story and ended up becoming a part of it.

Thank you Mike Carlomagno and John Peretto. When I was standing on the edge, your love and friendship pulled me back.

Thank you, Robert McGill. You stood up with me when no one else would, and it changed both our lives.

Thank you, Larry Rothstein and Sonny Poremba. West Valley is a better place because of both of you.

Thank you to Daniel L. Jensen, C.S.B. You saved my life, and I've spent the rest of it trying to show how thankful I'll always be.

And to every child I've ever taught: Thank you. You've blessed my life in more ways than I could ever express.

I'm a teacher of rejects: kids who've been rejected by parents who didn't want to take the time to raise them right or didn't know how to raise them; kids who've been rejected by schools because they weren't the highest achieving or the best athletes or the best behaved; kids rejected by society because they represented America's untouchable caste, the poor and the working poor.

Most of "my kids," as I think of them, live in overpriced, slummy apartments that house two or three times more people than were ever meant to live there. Frequently, they belong to a "patchwork family" that includes a combination of desperate, quasi-related young mothers who are barely in adulthood themselves; their children from a variety of men; thirty-to-forty-year-old gangster sons or brothers, either just released from prison or soon to be heading there; and the most dangerous family members of all, the rotating cast of new boyfriends, or "uncles." These men are commonly addicts or alcoholics who've been brought into the home because the kids' lonely, prematurely aging mothers are so desperate for male companionship that they close their eyes to reality and put their children at risk of physical and sexual abuse. This they do just to occasionally hear the words "I love you," after still another day of cleaning someone else's toilets.

Outside my students' homes lurk other dangers, other predators: all-purpose "scammers" who sell everything from bogus IDs and hot cell phones to stolen TVs, bootleg movies, porn, and any drug or weapon you desire. In a way these men and women have replaced the small drugs-only dealers. It's now a bizarro Wal-Mart scenario: one-stop shopping for all things illegal, illicit, and deadly.

And providing an ever-present, stressful background aroma of danger are the local gang members, always just an eerie "hood call" away, looking for weak and unsuspecting prey but just as often showing up in the crosshairs of unseen predators from other gangs who—slow, silent, evil—cruise the "hood" with headlights off, senses numbed by drugs and alcohol, and guns loaded, looking for a chance to settle the score with their rivals for some imagined slight.

WORST OF THE WORST

My kids are considered the worst of the worst: incorrigibles, chronic truants, criminals, compulsive graffiti taggers, drunks, and druggies. Some have stopped going to school for months, even years. Some have been expelled for fighting or bringing weapons to school. Many belong to neighborhood gangs and wear the usual colors of allegiance, red or blue. Some have spent a year or more in lockups for gang-related offenses. All of them, it would seem, are on the short list of life's early losers. In reality, they make the "career" choices that any child who has nothing might make. They escape from the tremendous stress and chaos in their lives by masquerading in society as ill-mannered, chronically mouthy adolescents.

Despite their trail of problems, when they walk in the door of West Valley Leadership Academy, in Canoga Park, California, if they really want to change their lives, we make a total commitment to love them. We protect them, make them behave and have respect for others and themselves, give them a code of ethics and values, sober them up, employ them, and reunite them with their families. Then we send them out the door healed, restored, and ready to live lives of purpose and fulfillment.

I contrast my students with an image of teenagers encouraged by many celebrities, especially young black media stars and athletes, and it's obvious which kids offend and victimize innocent folks. On television and in music these wealthy role models often promote rude, foul-mouthed "gangsta" behavior and appearance. Yet over the years my students, though racially mixed and in many cases ex-gangsters themselves, have learned to be respectful and considerate of others, regardless of skin color or cultural origins.

I raise the issue of this divide because the United States needs to begin a national conversation about which teenage attitudes and kinds of conduct are appropriate in public and which are just crude and obnoxious, certainly nothing to be encouraged by music, sports, and television celebrities.

CHALLENGE TO AMERICA

If Americans truly want to reverse the well-publicized crisis in our public schools, if they want to fight growing violence and improve academic performance, if they want to save lost, idle, and aimless children, then I propose a challenge: *Try my rules.* Enforce them and you will be attacking the *causes,* not the effects, of failure. Go after the *why* of kids' misbehavior, give them a foundation for making the right decisions. I have tamed hundreds of angry, violent children in this way. In most cases the change has taken root and held into adulthood.

This is not a naïve, pie-in-the-sky proposal and I'm not an idealist pounding particular faiths and prayers into young minds. Although I have my own faith, my teaching style is secular and targeted for practical results. Anyone can use my rules. I merely teach timeless, universal values.

My students learn traditional academic subjects, such as math and English composition, but integrity and character always come first. Unlike most schools—obsessed primarily with test scores, history dates, and correct comma placement—West Valley teaches moral or ethical principles, by means of my ten values-based rules, that will support people for the rest of their lives. My students come to me with enormous handicaps, yet they thrive—despite a spread in ages from thirteen to eighteen and an initial range in abilities from barely literate to college level.

For my rules proposal to work, there must be a shift of heart and commitment toward those we intend to help. Everyone, especially parents and educators, must participate. If teachers and principals ignore the rules, if they experience no sincere change of heart, if they do not return to the true mission of teaching, then they should not be toying with the lives of children; they should be tossed from the system before they further erode what was once a bedrock national resource.

Because daily student attendance generally determines how much income public schools receive, educators are understandably worried about growing absenteeism. Yet they seem to ignore why students (except those who are verifiably sick) don't want to attend. A major reason is that teachers continue their traditional approach: hours of often pointless, out-of-context, "drill-and-kill" sessions in which enthusiasm dies as academic factoids are rehearsed in a vacuum, all for the sole purpose of passing test after test. Most teachers know no other way.

Bored with trying to memorize this mostly soulless mass of knowledge, many students rebel and escape to drugs, alcohol, excessive promiscuity, gangs, and such mutant activities as choking games and torturous initiation rites. Schools, in effect, chase these kids away by boring them.

A BETTER WAY

In 2000, when a colleague and I started West Valley, a lot of my rules were merely suggestions. Our enrollment numbers fluctuated from twenty to more than thirty-five, depending upon the rate of referrals or requests from probation offices, schools unable to handle unruly kids, and desperate parents. At first, West Valley operated like an educational M.A.S.H. unit in a war zone. We'd get them to behave, patch up their academics, then send them back into the fray of mainstream schools, ready or not. Sometimes our remedies worked; sometimes they didn't.

Then, in January 2002, one of my students was shot in front of the school only minutes after class was dismissed for the day. It was a case of mistaken identity. The shooter drove by and fired point-blank at the boy, who had a typical gangster hairstyle and looked like the intended victim. The day after he died in my arms, I toughened the rules. I realized that weakly offered suggestions were no longer enough. Not only did I ban the current "gangster look" (shaved head, baggy pants, and oversized white T-shirt), but I also began enforcing every measure intended to protect students and keep them focused on changing their lives. Within three months, the results in behavior were spectacular:

- Daily attendance rose to nearly 100 percent.
- All students voluntarily tested for drugs, and tested clean.
- Violent and gang-related behavior disappeared.
- All students found jobs and were taking classes at either a community college or an occupational center.
- One hundred percent of our parents unfailingly showed up at our monthly meetings.
- Reading and math scores generally jumped in several months by an amount that normally would take several years.
- The graduation rate hit 80 percent, exceeding by at least 20 percent that of conventional public schools.

BASIC VALUES

To stay at West Valley, students, with the support of their parent or parents, must follow my rules. Some rules, like telling the truth or respecting others, have been around for millennia. They are basic to people trying to live together in harmony. To these rules I've added more specific ones to keep my students drug free and sober, employed in after-school jobs, and attending college or vocational classes elsewhere. Along with rules, the most important subject I teach, one that we *practice,* infuses every other subject, from algebra to zoology. This "subject" is a strong sense of values imbued with such qualities as love, honesty, courage, compassion, patience, and tolerance, as well as a positive attitude toward work.

We don't just talk about caring for someone other than ourselves. We pile on a bus and visit skid row shelters or nursing homes, where we clean and feed the unfortunate or just listen and learn from people who've already lived most of their lives. My students figure out how to stay alive with more than just memorized facts, academic skills, and earned diplomas. They also come to know what they're living for: to be contributors, givers and not just takers.

Of all the mottoes and verbal prods that adorn our school—formerly a small office building—one sign is dominant. We call it the academic success pyramid, which has three levels. Whatever my students do, it all begins with the foundation, the bottom level, with the four words "Integrity and Moral Courage." The next level up reads "Strong Work Ethic." At the top are the two payoff words, "Academic Achievement." For all of us, the pyramid is our mantra.

Our program does not make mere surface changes in our students' lives—it renews their hearts and souls. Those who come to us addicted leave us drug free. Those who walk in the door functionally illiterate and learning disabled walk out our door having passed college classes ahead of their peers. Those who enter West Valley alienated from their families—angry, selfish, and lost—usually exit with a strong sense of purpose, happy, eager to serve others, and reunited with their family circles. The change we work in our students' lives is so complete that visitors to our school often refuse to believe that these teenagers could ever have been considered "the worst of the worst."

LIGHTING THE WAY

It has taken me more than twenty-five years and a student dying in my arms, the casualty of a gang-related shooting, to develop a surefire way of turning around wayward kids. My approach saves money and works as easily for one bad kid as it does for one bad school—and several times I've turned around a school in under forty-eight hours. I believe that if I can get the best out of the worst, my methods can work for kids everywhere, incorrigible or not.

In the years since I tightened the rules, it hasn't always been sweetness and light. Pain and sacrifice were involved, but the students who stuck to the rules blossomed. Even the ones I suspended or dropped changed for the better. Often they continued at other schools, earned their diplomas, and went on to regular jobs, college, or the military. They still call or drop by, reminding me of this or that rule, some piece of quoted wisdom or guideline. They seem to carry with them certain rules not as platitudes but as torches to light their way, not as commands but as affirmations of inspired behavior.

It is in this spirit that I present my rules. For the most part they are straightforward guidelines that can be adopted and enforced by parents and schools in gradual stages and at little expense.

LIVING BY THE RULES

1. *We show up.* We show up in class on time every school day, just as we show up on time at work and at every other commitment we make.
2. *We dress right, we speak right.* We dress and speak appropriately for the place we're in and according to whatever the general practice or code indicates.
3. *We work.* We work mainly to earn money, gain skills and experience, improve our work habits and position, and sometimes just for the satisfaction of doing a good job.
4. *We tell the truth.* We tell the truth because honesty is the basis for all good and trusting relationships among people.
5. *We respect people and property.* We respect people and property because it's good common sense to keep the peace by treating others as you want to be treated.

6. *We live clean and sober.* We live clean and sober because drugs and alcohol are illegal for minors and are harmful to our health and safety, and sooner or later our drug or alcohol use becomes destructive to others.

7. *We live with courage.* We live with courage, which demands sacrifice, in order to reach our potential as people of moral character and integrity.

8. *We care.* We care about others because by giving back something of ourselves we improve the world of people around us.

9. *We learn from everything.* We learn about everything in order to become independent people of good character, integrity, and knowledge.

10. *We make a difference.* We make a difference by becoming respectful, law-abiding, working citizens who help make the world a better place.

LOVE AT FIRST SIGHT

I was a real screwup and couldn't talk to anybody about it. Now I can talk about my problems with Mr. White because he never leaves me alone until I do.

—Mike, 16, West Valley student; former gang member,
drug user, and high school dropout

Mark had the gangster look when he first came to West Valley in 2001. I was in my second year of finally running a program I had designed from scratch, and the school and its spruced-up site in Canoga Park, a community in the San Fernando Valley, was gaining a reputation as a model program for at-risk teenagers. It had taken me a couple of years to sell the program to my Los Angeles County Office of Education bosses and I was still tweaking the rules when Mark arrived.

At almost eighteen, Mark was slightly older than my average student, but he came with a typical history of *vida loca* (crazy life) habits and consequences: chronic truancy, drugs and fighting, and no idea of where he was going in life, certainly no purpose in mind beyond his own appetites for the day. He had been "officially" jumped (initiated) into a neighborhood gang but now regretted his decision and was trying to pull away from it. Lately, his gangster homies were harassing him and his family because he refused to actively participate in their mayhem.

On intake day, Mark, accompanied by his mother, came dressed in standard gang attire: baggy khakis and a long, white T-shirt. I saw him only at a distance, since Larry Rothstein, the school's probation officer, conducts the initial meeting with students and parents or guardians. Larry goes over our rules, tests the children's basic skills, and reviews their medical and academic history as well as any criminal or disciplinary records. I take over on the following day. At Mark's intake meeting, it seemed clear to Larry that the boy was coming to us to get away from the gang scene.

As with most new students, I deliberately avoided checking Mark's background because I didn't want to be prejudiced by his past behavior. At that point, Mark was tabula rasa to me. As usual, I planned to focus on what I believed existed behind the appearance and likely history of misdeeds. Corny as it might sound to some people, I would try to see the good in him and then build on that. Whatever I learned of his life, I hoped, would come from him in his own spoken or written words. Since I encourage self-disclosure, mine included, I was soon aware of his past gang ties, his minor offenses, and his pot smoking. Almost immediately I also found out he liked to do math problems but struggled with reading.

So I started tutoring him after class with his reading and I got to know a bit more. I knew he beamed in class at being one of the better math students, but beyond the satisfaction of zipping through equations, I thought he was drifting without purpose. I don't remember us ever talking in any depth about life after high school, about possible jobs or careers, even though I often brought up the subject in class. In fact, along with teaching values to kids, my main goal was and is to set them on track for an independent, employed future. But it appeared that Mark's ambitions were mostly to hang with his friends after school.

He was a charmer and his classmates liked him. But the kids who'd never been in or near gangs gave him a wide berth because of his previous ties to gangsters. Still, his easygoing, friendly manner helped him fit in with everyone. He took to calling me "coach" and started helping others with math problems. Since my students are of different ages and abilities, I encourage them to help each other, sharing their skills and wits, whether it's with long division or with a software program. I told Mark we were like a family, and he took to this aspect of the school without hesitation. Of course, he knew I could drop him for a number of different types of infractions, from smoking on campus to lying or fighting. No law compelled me to keep him if he didn't live up to our signed agreement.

Months passed, and I felt Mark wasn't making much progress on the road to an independent life. "We need to talk," I told him one day in the first week of 2002.

"Sure," he said, calmly running a hand over his bristly scalp. "Now?"

"After school, one-on-one."

"Oh," he said, frowning slightly and maybe realizing I had something serious in mind to discuss.

That afternoon, students dismissed, we sat down at a classroom table facing each other. "Mark," I began. "I'm worried about you."

"What do you mean?" he said, looking me straight in the eye.

"You know what I mean," I said in my all-business tone. "It's obvious in class that you're not doing anything worthwhile outside of school."

He tilted his head, waiting for me to continue.

"You should stop using drugs," I said, "get a job, grow your hair longer, and start preparing for your future."

For a moment he looked puzzled, then he gave me the little grin that in a boy eleven or twelve might have been sincere and charming but in a young man of almost eighteen had probably become a façade he used with me, his parents, and other adults he wanted to impress. I said a few more things but I could see he wasn't going to change anything in his life. I ended the meeting, thinking he had a strain of the "Peter Pan complex." He was fighting maturity; he didn't want to grow up beyond what he had been three or four years ago. And along the way no one had pushed him to change.

Less than twenty-four hours later, on the afternoon of January 8, 2002, just after I'd dismissed class, I was outside on the nearby corner checking out a rumor about a fight that was supposed to take place when I heard a loud boom that sounded like a cannon going off. I ran back toward the building, and a student yelled, "Mark's been shot!"

"Where is he?" I asked.

"He ran upstairs," the boy said. As I turned toward the school's front entrance, I noticed a puddle of blood on the sidewalk and a red trail leading inside. I ran up the stairs to my classroom, and there was Mark, slumped in a chair with blood on the front of his shirt. "Mark," I said, "you're going to be okay there? Why don't you lie down on the carpet?"

He looked at me blankly. He was in shock, and I was feebly trying to convince myself that his wound wasn't fatal. I told one of the kids in the hallway standing next to me to run to the restroom and bring back a wet paper towel to wipe his face. I helped Mark lie down on the carpet next to my desk and cradled his head and shoulders so I could hold him. He'd been shot once right through the chest. Feeling helpless, all I could do was watch as he bled onto the floor. In the seconds before life left him, I brought my face close to his and said, "We love you."

That evening, long after I called the police and called his parents, after everyone else had left the school, the last thing I did was wash Mark's blood off the sidewalk, then I cleaned it off the carpet in my office. Finally, I wiped the dried spots of blood off my computer.

MY EPIPHANY

By the following day, I'd found out from the police and several students who were eyewitnesses that Mark had been shot at close range by a gang member who mistook him for a rival gangster. The shooter was a passenger in a pickup truck that stopped long enough for a round to be squeezed off. No suspects were ever charged or arrested because the eyewitnesses feared for their lives, too—a typical response to gang threats or intimidation.

I also learned about a fight that I should have known about. It was supposed to have taken place after class let out the afternoon Mark was shot. Apparently everyone, including Mark, knew about the coming scrap between someone near our school and a kid who ran off to get some help and firepower from another neighborhood. If only somebody had come up to me that day in school and told me something—even a nonspecific rumor—of a problem, something like, "Mr. White, there's going to be a fight after school," I could have broken it up and Mark wouldn't have been a potential target. Sadly, no one warned me, and the result was tragic.

My students and I went to the tearful wake and funeral service, all of us wearing T-shirts commemorating Mark's name and life. At the Catholic church where a Mass for Mark was said, the priest offered me the chance to say something, but since I had so many mixed emotions at the time, I declined. I now regret not having spoken from the heart. I would have told all the gang members, friends, family members, and school staff in attendance that we needn't waste time looking for Mark's killer because in a way *we* were the killers. We all played a part in his death by not demanding he give up a lifestyle that, if it didn't end violently, we all knew could only end in death by drugs or disease, or in a life of poverty and alcoholism, fathering children he probably couldn't support because he'd be in prison or paralyzed from another gang shooting.

I would have said, "This slow kind of death would have been no less tragic than the shooting, only less sudden."

But I said nothing. Instead, I listened silently to the priest's well-intentioned homily, looked at the casket, and later tried to console Mark's grieving parents, seeing in their faces the worst kind of pain a mother and father can feel. Years later their tragedy continues; their wound hasn't closed because people have yet to finger the killer.

Mark's death triggered an epiphany in me: If I had been tougher on rule-breakers, if I had stopped *suggesting* so much and had started *enforcing* a zero-tolerance attitude toward transgressors, Mark might be alive. If I had forced him to grow his hair longer, he wouldn't have looked like a gangster, like a target. If I had tested him for drugs, I would have had a clear-minded student in class. If I had forced Mark to get a job, he wouldn't have been so idle and would have been earning money and self-respect. And if I had relentlessly pushed honesty and courage among the other students, I would have known about the corner fisticuffs after school. Suddenly, I saw what I had to do: tighten the rules.

MY FATHER AND MY CAREER

My journey toward creating my rules actually began in childhood. I didn't know it then, but my passion for teaching grew from the days when I would accompany my father, a life-long teacher in suburban Detroit, to the school where he worked. I was about ten, and on several occasions when I had the day off from my school, he took me with him to his own fifth-grade class. I'd sit with his students and I could tell immediately that he was in charge. He taught a homeroom class, covering all the basic subjects, although music was his specialty. He enjoyed being with the kids. He never raised his voice, never threatened them, but when he wanted order he got order. I think they sensed his inner conviction, because he always got their attention.

One time on our way home I told him I thought he was being too strict with the kids. "Paul," he said, "if you ever become a teacher, remember, you're not their buddy, their peer. You're there to give them something they don't have. You're there to move them to higher ground." I nodded, not fully comprehending. Years later, while earning a teaching degree from Eastern Michigan University, I knew that most of my ideas on how I would run a class would come from my father's example.

In 1974, when I was ready for my student-teaching assignment, my supervisor and classmates who'd already been in the field told me, "Never ask for a Detroit school or a junior high." They said that the best way to learn how to teach was to break into the profession gradually, with lots of support. But I was eager for a challenge and asked for a junior high school in Detroit. When I arrived at the school, I met my supervising teacher and watched her teach one day. On day two, she met me in her classroom, then left. I was on my own. I stepped into the noisy classroom and saw forty-five or so crazed adolescents, half of them out of their seats. It was love at first sight.

Among those kids was a boy named Kevin. He was about 5'7", slightly built, and very white. Most of his classmates were

African American. Kevin wasn't really unruly; he was just very angry. He was angry at the alcoholic father who'd left the family; angry at the mom who did menial work at a local store and was unprepared to support her four kids; angry that the family didn't have their own home and had to live with their grouchy grandfather; and angry that he had to live in a black neighborhood where he felt he had nothing in common with most of the kids. Kevin just felt he'd been doing his part and life had dumped on him.

At school or on the bus, the black kids would taunt him. He liked art, Elton John, and politics; they liked soul sounds, sexuality, and sports. Because of his anger and individualist streak, I sensed disaster in Kevin's future. To survive, he would either have to submit to the majority or find another way. I didn't know it then, but in helping Kevin find that other way and turn his life around, I took the first step in shaping a set of rules for saving young lives. I'll return to Kevin later, but first I want to mention the other schools that had a part in developing my approach. I also want to point out several other children whose stories illustrate how my teaching works.

After my semester of student teaching, I hungered for physical work outdoors. I left the classroom for construction work and eventually became a concrete contractor in Vallejo, California. I earned good money, but ultimately the job didn't satisfy my urge to teach kids, especially the out-of-control kind I was seeing more of on the streets. It was 1981 and I was newly married. My wife, Valerie, urged me to put down my wheelbarrow and follow my heart. So I walked into the personnel office of the local school district and came away with an eight-month temporary contract to teach the worst-behaved sixth-graders at Cave Elementary School.

Ornery and rebellious, they had already run off ten teachers in the first eight weeks of the school year. But I was also ornery and rebellious by nature. Whatever the antics or problems were, I would meet them head-on. On my first day with the students, I introduced myself as their new teacher. I wrote my name on the chalkboard, and then I went around the room asking names. Before the silent, wary looks faded, I asked them to write letters to me describing who they were. They wrote their letters and I collected them as they finished. I remember one boy wrote, "I have a very difficult time holding my temper when I get angry and I want to emphasize that!" I smiled and wondered when the first eruption would occur. I hadn't faced so many kids since my student-teaching time in Michigan. But I figured I could handle twelve-year-olds.

After I collected their letters, I turned to math, which was next in my neat little lesson plan, carefully worked out the night before. I would teach them how to divide fractions. I myself hadn't done fractions since my student-teaching days in college. So I wrote a problem on the board and worked it out, telling them what to do. Fortunately, I looked at a page in the answer book and saw that my answer was wrong. "Sorry," I said, erasing my numbers. "I made a mistake. Here's how you do it." I worked it out again, underlined the answer twice, and confidently turned to face the class. Just in case, though, I glanced down at the answer book, which was open on my desk. I was wrong again. "Sorry, kids," I said slowly through clenched teeth. "That's not the answer. You do it like this."

Facing the chalkboard for the third time and fighting back my own embarrassment, I could hear the kids starting to titter and giggle, as if to say, "Ha! He doesn't know how to divide fractions." On the verge of panic, I thought to myself, "Dear God, how *do* you divide fractions?"

Suddenly, I heard a shushing sound. I turned to see a pig-tailed little girl with one finger to her lips. She shushed the others again and then in a sweet, calm voice said, "Just give him time. Mr. White will get it."

I turned around and gave it another try. She was right. With a little time I worked out the correct answer. Appropriately enough, her name was Angel. After a few days, everyone fell in line and they began to like learning and being in a peaceful, orderly place. We got along so well that at the end of the year we all cried because the great ride was over. At Cave Elementary, I discovered I truly loved the cast-off kids other teachers couldn't handle or didn't want to try to teach.

The following year, Ellen Nims, the principal of Cooper Elementary, offered me my first full-time teaching job, which lasted from 1982 to 1987. I ended up with a class of the thirty-five worst kids in a school of about seven hundred students, which drew from a mixed-race working-class neighborhood. They were chronic bad apples, ages eight to twelve, all from the third to sixth grades. She believed that if anyone could control and teach them, surely a no-nonsense guy used to breaking concrete had a good chance.

But even with Ms. Nims's complete support and advice, I entered the classroom fray at some peril. One child assaulted me with a bike chain and then tried to bite and spit on me. Another urinated in my wastebasket. Still another stole money from me. One kid even sent his Hells Angels dad into the classroom to try and intimidate me.

After an initial adjustment period, I prevailed and went on to spend a delightful year with some wonderful students. I especially remember Peter. He was an eleven-year-old bundle of rage and confusion. He ditched class regularly and fought with everyone. His parents couldn't control him and apparently no one else could either. In class he'd sit off alone, involving himself with the other students only when he felt like it. The other kids would normally have teased and laughed at him, but Peter's reputation as a fighter limited them to socially isolating him.

How I "tamed" Peter into a polite and engaged student who wouldn't miss a class if he could help it is a story I'll leave for later chapters. For now, what's important to know is that Peter's success taught me that for children to show up for class, parents are the key. They, too, have to show up.

In Vallejo I learned to help minority and low-achieving, troubled children behave and be successful. Now I wanted to run a school myself and share what I'd learned with an entire faculty and community. While at Cooper Elementary, I had taken courses at the University of San Francisco and earned a master's degree in education administration, and now I wanted to use my new administration credential. I got my chance in a middle school in Valley Center, California, first as assistant principal, then as principal. What I didn't reckon on were the politics of running a school in a community where roughly half the students came from rich white families and the other half came from poor brown families, mostly Mexican and Indian. Basically, I was hired to take care of the haves and control the have-nots.

But I tangled with my bosses when I applied rules equally to all students, like the time I suspended the son of a white school board member for bringing a butterfly knife on campus. After two years of repeatedly bucking established norms, I decided to quit. The superintendent asked me to stay—after all, the academic test scores of racial minorities in the school were suddenly the highest in the school's history—but I was set on leaving. The lesson I learned at Valley Center was that sticking to principles pays off with kids and that waffling on principles sends a contradictory message to everyone, especially to children.

In 1989, I publicly announced that I wanted to run the worst possible school in California. Potrero Hill Middle School in San Francisco qualified, I interviewed for the job, and soon I became its principal. When I arrived for work the place was in full meltdown: substance abuse, inappropriate sexual acts, nonstop profanity, the showing of porn films, vandalism, violent attacks were rampant—and this was just among the staff, many of whom refused to work. The 650-plus students, of course, thrived on misbehavior.

Six weeks later, working more than ninety hours a week and averaging one wrestling match per day with one or another unimaginably out-of-control child, I survived to see Potrero as a model of well-behaved, well-performing students and faculty. To bring about this transformation I had had to enforce all the normal regulations that had been ignored or winked at for years. Unfortunately, eight days before the end of the school year, my superintendent decided that supporting my efforts to improve the school apparently wasn't worth risking the ire of the teachers' union and his career. He surprised me by informing me my contract would not be renewed.

Though I was now out of a job, I realized that by enforcing rules in the educational code I could quickly turn around one delinquent student, or hundreds. Success had little to do with numbers and everything to do with the principle of following the rules. Looking for a way to test my approach even further, I designed a plan to recruit and reform San Francisco's worst dropouts imaginable, all teenagers older than those of middle-school age. With financial backing primarily from Fritz Maytag of the appliance-company family, I started a nonprofit called Project Star with a group of ten hard-core offenders, including car thieves, drug addicts and dealers, drive-by shooters, and an alleged murderer.

I worked them hard and, above all, relentlessly pushed character values over academics. It worked, and the boys turned around their dead-end lives and earned high school diplomas in four months instead of the projected six. Later, some of them continued in college and all stayed employed and out of the criminal life. My experiment in reforming genuine hard-core offenders gave me the foundation for the rules I use today.

In 1991, Valerie and I moved south, to Ventura County,

where I was hired as principal of the Ventura County Courts Schools. The job allowed me to try out my methods and values-based approach on convicted and jailed teenage boys and girls. I was supposed to educate them with the hope that they wouldn't commit crimes again. Within days I discovered I had walked into a program that was grossly out of compliance and fiscally mismanaged. I wrote a report for my new bosses showing how we could correct all the educational-code violations. The district administrator saw the report as potentially very damaging to him, immediately removed me from my position as principal, and told me I could quit with a partial payoff or accept a demotion and finish the contract year as a teacher. I chose the latter and became an independent-study teacher. For three years, I honed my skills in redirecting the lives of my high-risk students. Later, my bosses faced legal charges for their fiscal and managerial misdeeds, and the county office of education had to pay out big money in fines and lawsuits.

By then I had gone on to start up a charter school near San Luis Obispo for about one hundred K-through-six children, followed in 1998 by a return to teaching hard-core delinquent teens in Los Angeles at Mid-Valley Community Day School, which is one of scores of similar facilities that Los Angeles County runs to handle their most difficult adolescent boys and girls, the ones regular schools can't handle.

I think of Mid-Valley as my monster school. The place was filthy, covered with graffiti, and overrun with cockroaches. Most of my sixty or so students, whom I split with two other teachers, were gang members and drug dealers. Two different students assaulted me during my first two days, but gradually I managed to get the students to pay attention to my rules, especially the one about respecting people and property.

One of my first turnarounds was a tough teenager named Carlos. The day I first walked into the classroom, I saw him at the back of the class giving me the hard stare. He'd already done almost two years in juvenile halls and youth camps for serious felonies, and statistics would suggest that he was destined for prison or an early death in a gang shooting. Thickly built, he unnerved most adults because of his unflappable manner. In a roomful of streetwise and rough incorrigibles, Carlos looked the most threatening. Trying to psych out other gang members, he would even speak in a gravelly kind of voice à la Marlon Brando in *The Godfather*. The other kids wouldn't mess with him, but I never bought the act. To me the back-row Godfather was just trying to be darkly funny, seeing who could be intimidated and who could not. That first day I had seen the real Carlos and just knew we would get along.

DOING WHAT'S REQUIRED

In 2000, when I moved to the West Valley facility, it seemed the final pieces were in place for a master education plan that could be used by all educators for all kids. The next year, when Mark died in my arms, I made the last adjustment to my rules: I tightened them.

Winston Churchill wrote that sometimes it's not enough that we do our best—we must do what's required. Similarly, I realized after Mark was shot that if I couldn't take my approach further, couldn't put teeth into my rules, couldn't do more than just keep the kids from going wild, then all my efforts were futile. I decided to have a school program that would truly change lives, overnight if possible. If I failed to put a backbone in what we were doing at West Valley, then I'd shut the door and walk away. It wasn't worth having a school with spineless rules.

I tightened the rules by focusing on the consequences for breaking them. Suddenly, the rules had no gray area. For the kids it was all or nothing, and attending West Valley even for one day was a big deal. In a sense, I treated the students more like adults, giving them choices. Essentially, I told them, "Either you're in or you're out; you follow the rules or you don't. If you choose to violate what we do here, fine. No hard feelings but you're out. You can come back when you're ready to join us and we'll see if it's possible. Or you can try transferring to a regular high school or to another alternative program. Just remember, if you try to live without strong rules, your possible outcomes are bleak; going back to drugs and alcohol, or poverty, hustling on the street until you end up in prison, or dead before you're twenty."

A Time Line of My Teaching Career

Detroit, 1974: Student teacher. I follow my father's example.

Vallejo, California, 1981: Cave Elementary School teacher. I love working with the kids others can't handle.

Vallejo, California, 1982–87: Cooper Elementary School teacher. I pull in the parents to participate.

Valley Center, California, 1987–89: Valley Center Middle

School assistant principal and principal. I stick to principles and it pays off.

San Francisco, 1989–90: Potrero Hill Middle School principal. I discover that turnarounds happen when I enforce the rules.

San Francisco, 1990–91: Founder and director of Project Star dropout recovery program. I develop the foundation for my rules.

Ventura, California, 1991–94: Principal, then teacher in the Ventura County Courts Schools. I hone my skills redirecting the lives of troubled kids.

San Luis Obispo, California, 1996–97: Principal and teacher of Bellevue–Santa Fe Charter Elementary School. I start a school from the ground up.

Los Angeles, 1998–2000: Teacher at Mid-Valley Community Day School. I tame the "monster" school of incorrigibles by perfecting my rules.

Los Angeles, 2000–present: Teacher at West Valley Leadership Academy. I discover the lasting benefits of strongly enforcing the rules.

Rule #1

WE SHOW UP

I remember I was a couple of minutes late and I was sent home. At the bus stop I was thinking that if I really wanted to change my life I couldn't be late. It wasn't going to happen again.

—Jason, 16, West Valley student,
former drug addict and gang member

It sounds easy enough: Show up on time. Miss class or show up late without an acceptable excuse—say, a trip to the ER—and I send you home, suspend you, or maybe drop you from the program, depending upon the circumstances. "It's like a job," I tell them. "You make a habit of not showing up, you lose your job." To those I send home I usually add, "When you're ready, come back and we'll talk." Many do come back, and they stay. They thrive because they commit to the rules, starting with coming to school on time, every morning.

For them that's not easy. Many come from other parts of Los

Angeles and have to catch a bus before 6 A.M. in order to cross a big chunk of the city and arrive on time. Even if they live closer to the school and don't have to spend two hours on the bus to get to class, they must somehow leave behind the temptations of a world where, for many, vandalism is seen as just a harmless diversion, not a real crime; where drug and alcohol use is one of the few activities the whole family shares; where buying stolen goods is a wise way to stretch the family budget; where the police are an irritant interrupting the flow of these activities; and where preteen sexual activity, getting arrested, and gang membership are rites of passage.

So when I see them arrive on time every morning, I see my heroes. Somehow they make it to class, even after mopping floors at McDonald's until 11 the night before. Tired and sleepy, they know that "showing up" is much more than a matter of punctuality and perfect attendance. For those who stay with the program, showing up becomes a normal attitude and habit for doing everything, from saying the magic words "please" and "thank you" to keeping appointments for job interviews to laboring over a set of algebra equations.

The show-up-or-get-dropped rule seems harsh, especially for kids unused to rules and limits, but the hard-line approach works. Timely attendance is perfect nearly every day. In many schools, skipping a class or playing hooky for the entire day hardly raises eyebrows. College-bound students from intact middle-class families can ditch and no one seriously believes absences will keep them from attaining degrees, good jobs, or professional careers. Even illegal handicaps such as drug addiction are usually seen as treatable, temporary setbacks.

But teaching children, rich or poor, to wink at violations of any rule does far more harm than educators and parents realize. As I tell my students, the rule on timely attendance is really about the underlying values, about maintaining the only beliefs in life that have any real worth. Obeying rules is about maintaining your honesty (not lying to your parents or teachers or both about why you were late or absent). It's about maintaining your integrity (lying in any area of your life will ultimately spread to all areas of your life). And finally, obeying rules is about maintaining a principle of democratic republics: No one is above the law. In my experience this last principle needs to be taught more emphatically in affluent schools, because the children there have learned the dangerous philosophy that moral ends justify the use of immoral means.

This doesn't mean you teach children that the only two choices in life are mindless obedience to archaic rules or continued deceit. You teach the constitutional premise that when laws no longer serve the best interests of an organization, its members have the responsibility not to break but to change the laws. If educators believe that everyone coming to school at a certain time helps students, then they must have the conviction to enforce the rule. If the rule seems arbitrary and doesn't work, then they should change the rule to something that does (flex-time, for example). Running a school this way takes more work than just letting students lose respect for all the rules, but it's worth the effort. In the long run, I tell educators and parents alike, this commitment to honesty and respect for law will leaven and improve every relationship and activity in your school.

My students can't afford to play with the rules. One or two no-shows or late-shows with lame excuses and everything can collapse. Within minutes a kid who's gone from being a hard-core gangster punk to a courteous young gentleman can find himself out on the sidewalk in front of the school with nothing but time to think about what he's lost. He's not used to being called on something he's been doing for years. He thinks it's no big deal. He may even feel victimized. But he and I both know that he's been bending or breaking some of my other rules all along. Arriving late or calling in sick are just symptoms of a lot more going wrong in his life. Whatever the reason, he broke his word that he would show up. He violated a simple, straightforward promise he made to the school the day we accepted him. So I drop him.

PETER SHOWS UP AND TURNS AROUND

Twenty years ago, at Cooper Elementary in Vallejo, I was only starting to come up with firm rules for my class of troublemakers. As the designated heavy taking all the troublesome kids from the third, fourth, fifth, and sixth grades, I received thirty-five boys and girls from other, much-relieved, teachers who had given up on trying to control them. Of all my incorrigibles, my embittered little fourth-grader, Peter, presented the toughest attendance challenge. He continually showed up late to class or didn't come at all.

Peter sat off by himself, a bundle of rage who took offense at just about any remark or look directed his way. His reputation as a fighter was the only thing that kept at bay what normally would have been merciless teasing prompted by his poor reading ability. But I still kept an eye on the situation. On the small side for eleven, he was afraid of nothing and no one. The day he was brought into my class, he had just finished lashing out at his teacher, calling him a "faggot" for allowing other kids to laugh at him because he couldn't do a lesson.

Peter's main problem was his abysmal reading ability, a source of continual frustration. His mom and dad spoke Spanish at home, which no doubt affected his English writing and reading ability. He lagged so far behind the others that I placed him in what I called Reading Group 1: its two members being him and me. Predictably, he fell back on old habits, ditching class or arriving late. I then decided that before I lost him completely, I would try an all-out assault on his poor attendance. I would take him to and from school and I'd tutor him before and after class. This meant arriving at his home a little after 6:30 A.M. and bringing him to Cooper with me. After school, I'd tutor him for a few more hours, and then I'd drive him back to his house. I would not give him an excuse to miss class. I would make him my special project.

Luckily, his father, a construction laborer, and mother gave me free rein with their son's schooling, since they had no idea what to do with him. His father, especially, understood when I explained that children are like pouring new concrete, something I had had years of practice doing. After you pour it in the form, you have only a limited amount of time to determine its final shape, to move it around, work it, tamp it, and protect it while it dries. Likewise, parents and teachers only have a certain amount of time to shape their children's character and behavior.

What we all knew was that if we didn't do some serious shaping now with Peter, he was on course to join his two older brothers in the youth prison system. And we all wanted to keep him from such a fate. The first day I picked him up, I told him, "I'll get you to class, but you're going to have to work hard, behave yourself, and quit the fighting. Do you understand?" I think he respected my directness and no-nonsense manner because he quickly nodded, and that's how our pact began.

In the summer, when I was attending college classes for my permanent credentialing, I would drive to Peter's house before 7 A.M. and tutor him at his family's kitchen table for an hour. Together, we would then drive to my college campus. While I was in class, he'd wait outside in the hallway studying on his own. I even took him along on my moonlighting jobs pouring concrete, giving him pin money for doing little chores like washing tools at the sites. He would also join my wife and me for occasional meals at our house, which were always preceded by more tutoring.

Soon Peter's anger started to die, kids no longer laughed at him, and he stopped fighting. Gradually, he began to catch up to the other kids in reading and writing. Subjects engaged him and he got pats on the back for hard work. In the end he truly liked showing up for class. His enthusiasm confirmed what I already knew instinctively: kids are more likely to want to come to school when they're successful and feel that someone cares about them.

Of course, if Peter's parents had not cooperated with me, his turnaround might never have happened. Cooper Elementary was where I learned that parents had to support everything I did. I formed pacts with parents, as I did with Peter's parents, not only to get them to attend meetings and other activities but also to back my rules.

ZERO TOLERANCE WORKS

Public schools seldom if ever follow a zero-tolerance approach to tardiness and truancy. Even without zero tolerance, I suggest they can quickly reverse a bad situation by not allowing stragglers on campus, by making sure school grounds and hallways are empty when the tardy bell rings, and by counseling chronic offenders. If these truants and habitual latecomers continue to defy attendance rules, they should be dropped, as state laws and school district regulations allow. I also believe administrators who are unable to achieve these attendance goals should be dismissed and replaced.

But to achieve near or perfect 100 percent attendance, as we do at West Valley, parents must enforce their own 100 percent rule. I probably would have failed in helping Peter change his attitude toward school if his parents had not backed me up. Where rules are concerned, parents set the example. Kids generally do what they're allowed to do. If little or nothing attracts them about school and if no one comes down on them hard when they ditch or skip, the behavior continues. Such children often become adults who lie, cheat, avoid steady work, abuse drugs and alcohol, and are anything but educated people of good character.

If parents know or suspect that their children skip classes a lot, they should talk to teachers, ask to observe classes, listen and watch. The kids will most likely object to this, but they'll know their parents are truly concerned about their schooling and that they don't want them being idle, hanging with friends off campus, or possibly committing crimes. Sons and daughters may whine about boring classes, but as long as the school is a clean and safe place to attend, parents must support attendance rules. Unfortunately, many schools are not clean and safe. If fear and disgust with the conditions prompt kids to avoid school, then it's up to parents collectively to pressure school leaders and elected officials to enforce rules against violence, intimidation, and vandalism.

RUNAWAY MOM

When parents don't show up to support me in teaching their children, I try to find out why and make them see that we're allies. Sometimes I go to extreme lengths to make this happen. It's that important. Once, about the same time I was working with Peter, I wanted to chat with a particular single mom who was determined not to talk to me, let alone form a pact with me. In fact, she would literally run away whenever she saw me heading toward her. I'd been tutoring her son, Alan, a fourth-grader, after school, and all I wanted to do was discuss his progress. But she always managed to evade me. It was as if she had Paul White radar. She'd spot me across the parking lot or at the end of a hallway, and she and Alan would trot over to their minivan, hop in, and speed away. Or if I did catch her within earshot, she'd say, "Sorry, I don't have time!"

I spent many afternoon hours with Alan, who was

overindulged and lazy, and my patience was about to snap. After all, he was *her* son. She should have been seeking *me* out. So one afternoon I saw her leaving the school and I went after her into the parking lot. As usual she ignored my calls to stop, breaking into a run with her son. The two scrambled into the minivan and off they raced, tires squealing.

I bolted for my pickup truck, got in, and gave chase. When she saw me catching up with her, she must have floored it, accelerating far above the speed limit. Heedless of cops, we went weaving in and out of traffic through downtown Vallejo, speeding down main thoroughfares and side streets. It was crazy and dangerous but I just couldn't let her get away. We had to talk.

Finally, she made a wrong turn, into a cul-de-sac, and I pulled in behind her, blocking the minivan. She had nowhere to go. I took a deep breath, slid out of my pickup, and walked over to the car. The window on the driver's side was lowered to reveal a young woman with tired eyes and a strung-out, jumpy manner. "All right, Mr. White, you win," she said. "What do we need to talk about?"

"Him," I said, indicating Alan.

"What about him?"

"You're babying him too much. You're his mother and if you don't start pushing him to work harder, both of you are going to regret it for the rest of your lives."

She looked at me as if I'd thrown cold water on her face. I'd heard she might have been abusing drugs, so I figured she was being easy on him out of some kind of addiction guilt. "You feel sorry for him, but that's not going to help him in class," I told her.

"Okay," she said. "What do you want me to do?"

She listened to me, less jumpy now, and agreed to tighten up on her son. She even said she'd drop by the next day for another conference. She showed up as promised, and from then on she came to all the school's parent-teacher meetings, to our one-on-one chats, and to any other activities parents could attend. Her son also dropped his lethargic, bored attitude and his class work improved.

Today at West Valley I no longer chase moms at high speed, but I still demand constant parent involvement. I make sure all parents, whether they're single, remarried, or just loosely attached, know that everything begins with showing up, not just their kids but them as well. As a public school whose mission is to reform and educate delinquent kids, we make this very clear at the orientation we give parents when we screen new applicants. Some adult in the child's life must attend the monthly parent-teacher meetings. It's a rule, not a suggestion, and there are consequences for missing these evening gatherings. If a mother, father, or designated family adult fails to appear at such a meeting, with few exceptions I will drop the student. In this way, I hold parents even more responsible for observing the show-up-or-else rule than I do their children. After all, parents are the adults and they should know better. If they don't understand this, I remind them of it every chance I get. Too much is at stake. One misstep on their part, one too many beers after work, one forgotten appointment, and their kid's future can easily head south.

NOLA BREAKS FREE

For too long Nola's parents didn't care about her education. They certainly never pushed her to excel in school. In other circumstances, she might have been scholarship material for the country's elite universities. When she came to West Valley, I could see that she wanted to learn, despite a family environment that included drug abuse and gang involvement. Much like Peter, she was tough physically, but I also sensed that she possessed an inner mental toughness.

Almost six feet tall, athletic but a bit out of shape, Nola grew up having to maneuver around drug-dealing in her home. She had a disarming smile and an almost bashful manner, and she always wore two necklaces. A Tinker Bell pendant dangled from one necklace, and a fearsome-looking Oakland Raiders insignia hung from the other necklace. In a way the Disney figure stood for the ultimate ideal of how she would have liked to remain: a perpetual little girl, light, happy, and problem free. Just sprinkle magic dust and she could effortlessly soar above and away from all things dangerous or undesirable. The other necklace with the sinister image of a barbarian football pro expressed how Nola actually had grown up. In her San Fernando Valley 'hood, the Raiders logo meant just one thing: I'm down with the gangs.

Nola's family was very poor. Her father and mother were from Mexico and had received very little formal education. Essentially, they were goodhearted people who in their way loved their only child, but the temptation of quick money from dealing drugs was just too much for them to withstand. Abandoning this lifestyle became even more difficult when Nola's father developed a severe medical condition that made it almost impossible for him to do any physical labor.

As a small child, Nola was naturally bright and liked going to school. But every morning as she got ready for school, she would have to tiptoe around Dad as he slept off the long nights of drugs and boozing. Her childhood days were spent walking home along blocks of noisy, chaotic, gang-infested apartments, then picking her way around drunken and drug-stupefied gang members hanging out in her living room getting high with her dad. Amid the combined blare of *ranchera* and rap music, she would try to concentrate on her homework; if she hit a difficult problem, she had to figure it out on her own.

She held her own in school for most of her elementary years, despite some learning time that was lost when she was quite young when her parents took her back to Mexico for an extended stay. Nola's world started to unravel just prior to entering puberty. The junior high school coursework was now more difficult to do on her own, and she quickly fell in with the negative habits of all her girlfriends. She also took up drugs, truancy, and the promiscuous, gangster lifestyle. With no one to point her in another direction, the effects of peer pressure were too great and she joined *la vida loca*.

Nola showed up at West Valley after several years of this hard living, and she wore the effects of it. To vent the anger she felt toward her parents, she had become a real brawler. While she still had high intellectual aptitude, she lagged far behind in credits from missing so much school. Years of bingeing on alcohol and drugs had broken her down physically, and she was very fragile emotionally. Battling depression and a hair-trigger temper, she was referred to us by an independent-study program that she had enrolled in because the gangster lifestyle was losing its once-glamorous appeal for her. Her instructor believed she would benefit from our program.

Nola had grown tired of spending hours on weekends waiting in line to visit her felony-convicted "homies" at the county jail. Repeat trips to the hospital to see the most recent *vato*—street dude—who'd been shot or stabbed also became more and more disturbing. As she sat through the hysteria and horror of repeated gangster funerals, it became clear to her that the wasted lives, despair, and premature deaths she was seeing could someday become features of her existence and she, too, could end up in a coffin if she didn't change her ways.

She decided to break free and see if there was any way she could rekindle her previous love of learning in school. Wearing her Tinker Bell and Raiders necklaces, Nola showed up at West Valley determined to change her life. As I show later, her parents played a key part in her fight to break free of her past.

Schools

- Enforce a zero-tolerance rule against stragglers on the campus.
- Do the same for students outside classrooms after the tardy bell rings.
- Counsel chronic tardy or absent students about their behavior and drop them if they fail to comply.

- Dismiss and replace administrators unable to achieve attendance goals.

Parents

- Enforce a 100-percent-attendance rule. Deny your children privileges or money; do whatever it takes, but stay firm and stay connected to the school.
- Talk to teachers, observe classes. Find out what's going on, and why your child skips class or shows up late.

Rule #2

WE DRESS RIGHT,
WE SPEAK RIGHT

I was into drugs, drinking, and failing. I was out of
school eighty percent of the time. I came here and I
couldn't wear gang colors and they tested for drugs.
But that was cool because they were all about respect.

—Albert, 20, U.S. Navy Reservist, and college student;

West Valley graduate

We dress right, which means we have the following dress
code at West Valley: plain gray or black T-shirts and
sweatpants, black or white sneakers, and socks—nothing blue
or red (gang colors) and no exceptions. As for speech, the rule
seems as simple and straightforward as having to wear gray
sweats: Speak respectfully and avoid profanity.

After a bit of wincing, most newcomers adjust to dressing
this way and to the ban on the likely four-letter words. But as
with the show-up-or-else rule, there's more to it than that.
These rules carry the following warning, included in the agree-

ment they and their parents or guardians sign before I accept them: "Anything that is spoken, done, implied, written, or worn that promotes gang affiliation is against the law and will result in immediate discipline, including possible arrest and removal from the campus by the police." Directed mainly to the boys, this means no shaved heads (a gangster style), no visible boxer shorts, and no gang gestures, postures, logos, or anything with the gang colors, red and blue.

Since I stiffened the penalty for dress-code violations after Mark died in my arms, I've dropped many students for what outsiders might consider minor missteps. For example, I tossed one sixteen-year-old boy for dangling a red thread from the pocket of his sweatpants. A Blood gang member, he made a choice to defy the ban on red. He was trying to challenge a new kid, who had ties to the Crip gang. A piece of shiny red thread hanging from a pocket may not seem like much—teachers at most schools, even big-city minority schools, wouldn't even notice a dangling red thread, let alone give a warning about it. But at West Valley we sweat the small stuff: a red thread or other gang sign could easily cause someone's death at our school; it did the afternoon a drive-by shooter blasted Mark because he looked like a certain gang member.

"Some thugs," I tell the class, "are cruising the neighborhood high out of their minds just looking for a possible rival, someone dressed like one. And if we happen to be outside on the noon break, they just might drive by in the alley. One of them aims a forty-five out the window, and *pow!* One of us crumples to the ground and dies on the spot. So if you believe I'm making the hard call on the thread thing, that I'm unfair, think again. These kind of guys kill innocent people almost every day somewhere in the country."

The Blood I dropped from the program was a typical case of repeatedly testing me on little things, until I finally called him on it. The dangling thread was the culmination of other bad choices he had made.

In part we have rules to eliminate the gang look because of who and where we are. But there are good reasons to impose dress codes at all schools, even those without gang problems. Only at the most basic level is "dressing right" about prohibiting gang attire as well as promiscuous-appearing clothing for girls. This rule doesn't move a school ahead; it simply eliminates the most obvious magnets for violence and disruption. It calms down the campus atmosphere so that teachers and administrators can focus on the real issues, on the values beneath the appearance. But as with all rules, for a conservative dress code to succeed, affluent and blue-collar parents alike must cooperate. Without bucking mainstream fashion too much, they can tell their teenagers to dress in public as if they were applying for jobs: Be neat and presentable.

Consistent, neutral dress for boys during their adolescent years discourages unproductive aggressiveness or "preening." There is a similar plus for girls: encouraging modesty in their dress code allows them to "blame it on" the rules that they are not able to wear revealing, provocative clothes to school. They are thus freed from much of the leering by boys as well as the sexually obsessed interaction among kids that drags down a school's entire learning atmosphere. Students at schools with such dress restrictions, though they may not be aware of it, also learn positive values such as respect for authority, humility in team efforts, and acceptance of others on the basis of deep, not superficial, qualities.

Typically, visitors to West Valley see respectful, sober students sitting sweetly in class, working busily over binomials, reciting short-story passages, or quietly composing essays on computer screens—not shouting or talking loudly, not chewing gum, not crinkling paper, not snoozing. All eyes are focused on me or on the lesson at hand. When visitors see such a scene, it's easy for them to forget that before I met my students they were not in the habit of following rules about proper appearance, behavior, and speech.

CARLOS AND MY "MONSTER" SCHOOL

At Mid-Valley Community Day School, the place I call my "monster" school, Carlos was the unflappable, glaring kid intimidating others with his Brando-Godfather imitation. Like many of the students, he came from a hard-core gang background and had served a total of nearly two years in juvenile detention facilities for assault and other felonies. Although I got Carlos and the other students to shed most of their baggy-clothes and bald gangster appearance, changing their deeper gang attitudes and lifestyle was a much greater challenge. The turnaround tale of my "monster" school and its students begins with appearance, both theirs and the school's.

Physically, Mid-Valley was the worst school I'd ever seen. I first saw it just before the Fourth of July weekend in 1998. I had

arrived to take over an alternative school for about sixty delinquent teenagers in the Los Angeles County city of Van Nuys. I
was to run the program and share the teaching load with two
other instructors. The place, which had been a small medical
building, looked like a trash heap, with broken windows; graffiti and carvings on practically every surface; food and candy
stuck to the walls; filthy, littered floors; grimy, gum-covered
carpets; stopped-up toilets and urinals; a cesspool stench; and
cockroaches and flies everywhere. So much food had been
stuffed in the desks by previous students that the first day I was
continually batting away flies from my face.

As for my charges, who sat or slouched in front of me, they
looked on with alternately bored and bemused expressions, a
motley group of twenty-five or so kids: mostly African American and Latino, along with some Asian and white kids. A newly
instituted dress code of sweat clothes was moderately in effect,
but before walking in the door and immediately after leaving,
most of the boys wore sagging, baggy pants or below-the-knee
Dickies, T-shirts, assorted head wraps, and ball caps, while
most of the girls sported shorts that were too small, tank tops,
and a lot of jewelry. The guys, almost all with shaved heads,
were virtually all gang members. The girls, with their big hoop
earrings and overdone makeup, resembled (and sometimes
were) hookers and strip-club dancers.

"Good morning," I said, entering the classroom for the first
time. "I'm Paul White, your new teacher." In the silence I noticed a few shrugs, some glares, and a lot of open mouths as if
to say, "What's this?" I stood behind my desk at the front of the

classroom, one hand waving at flies like a windshield wiper. I continued: "I'm here to teach and I'm going to tell you how I'm going to do it. I'm also going to clean up the place."

Somebody chuckled as a cockroach dropped from the ceiling onto my lesson plan. The quarter-size creature got its bearings, then disappeared over the edge of the desk. "We're going to say the pledge of allegiance," I said. "Please stand."

I waited a few moments, expecting some of the students to stand. "Come on. We're going to do this."

They remained seated, unmoved. For years, I had seen such defiance at the other places where I had taught delinquent kids: jailhouse classrooms, alternative programs, schools whose teachers readily gave me their worst malcontents to reform. From the beginning I had always connected with the trouble-makers, the ones other teachers couldn't handle. I had a knack for turning them around. As a teacher and administrator I had been developing an approach that worked well in a public-school setting. I was still tinkering with the rules, but overall I thought my methods were on target. I was eager to try them out on my latest reclamation project, despite the awful conditions.

I knew the drill. Sullen gangster attitudes were all too famil-iar. The kids would test the new guy, try to provoke him, try to shoot down his confidence. Scare the teacher out of the school, push him into not caring, and force him to run away. It was al-ways the same and I thought I was ready to take them on. Whatever they tried, I felt I could prevail. I would tame them.

So I repeated my request in a calm, deliberate voice, "We're going to do this. Please stand and face the flag." The dusty piece of red, white, and blue cloth drooped from a stick angling out from the wall behind me. In the back row, the boy I would know as Carlos raised his chin and looked away, probably feigning boredom but more than likely wondering how I'd handle defeat.

I waited. "By the way," I said. "We're going to do this every morning. And there'll be some rules you'll have to follow." I mentioned a few, like coming to school on time every day, no cussing, no lying, no marking up the walls. After a few head shakes and smiles, a big girl with a menacing frown cocked her head and spoke: "Yeah, we heard that before, heard it from every other teacher that's come through here."

"Well, I'm not them," I said. "Things are going to be different."

The girl raised an eyebrow. "Whatchu gonna change around here?"

I paced behind the desk, still waving away flies. "This weekend, Fourth of July," I explained, "I'm going to come in and fix it so we'll have a place we can be proud of."

"We'll see," the girl said, suddenly serious. "You say you care and that you're going to fix the place up."

"That's right," I answered, glancing around at the other faces. They seemed curious about the fresh meat in their midst.

"You do that?"

"You've got my word."

The girl raised her eyes to the ceiling, probably counting the roaches. "Well, you show me a place that looks decent and I'm in. You can count me in."

With that, she rose from her seat and looked at the flag. Slowly, begrudgingly, the others stood, even Carlos. I remember

39

reciting the pledge, hearing voices stumble after me, thinking I had jumped the first hurdle in getting these kids turned around. As it happened, that was the easiest test of the day. Before long I had to wrestle my way out of one boy's choke hold, drag him into the hallway, and ultimately push him out the front door. When I returned, I found another boy riffling through my desk. I told him to leave or I'd have to throw him out, too. He was eighteen, a big kid and a convicted felon, and he threatened to seriously hurt me. I called the police and they arrested him. Later I testified against him in court and the judge gave him a six-month sentence.

As usual, in both cases the bullies had held the others hostage, intimidating them with threats, tough-guy swagger, and a reputation for violence. Once they were gone, once they saw I was willing to back up my words, serious trouble dropped and soon disappeared.

But I still had to show up on the weekend for the school's facelift. Fortunately, my wife and a former troubled student I'd turned around pitched in. We hosed out the restrooms, put up mirrors, scraped and scrubbed the hallways and classrooms, disinfected desks, replaced broken light fixtures and windows, painted walls, even rolled five gallons of brown paint onto my classroom's ugly carpet.

Forty-eight hours after I began the makeover, students arrived in trickles, each one gazing around, poking into the restrooms, checking the walls, sniffing the air, amazed at the transformation. That morning I told them I could change them, too, clean them up, make them proud, give them reasons to live, teach them to be winners. All they had to do was follow my rules. "What do you say?" I asked them.

"All right, Mr. White," said the big girl who had broken the ice on my first day, "I'm in."

"Good," I said. "Now let's say the Pledge of Allegiance." Everyone stood, we recited the pledge, and that was the beginning of the end of my "monster" school.

Several weeks later, on a field trip to Malibu and the beach, we were approached by two well-dressed women who had been watching the group. They were impressed by how polite and well spoken the kids were and by how neatly they were dressed. They wanted to know what private school they attended and what the tuition amount was. I said the kids were public school students, many with criminal records, and they came from some nasty L.A. neighborhoods. The women looked doubtfully at the kids, who no longer looked like gangsters and hookers. They wore sweats, jeans, and T-shirts. The women asked me more about the school and I obliged. At one point they asked how I got the kids to attend willingly every day. "They show up," I said, "basically because they like it."

"Of course, that makes sense," the woman said. She smiled, apparently satisfied, said good-bye, and walked off.

Carlos gradually dropped his intimidating demeanor. He was a capable student and he liked that I was polite and friendly with him. I made it clear I was in charge and that if he didn't want to respect that, he'd have to go. He stayed, at least on the surface agreeing to my rules. I believe he stuck with the class initially because he sensed I truly cared about him. He also knew I was willing to mix it up with any students who even implied they might consider physically assaulting me. At a school where we ran metal-detecting searches every morning, followed by a sweep in the bushes near the entrance for stashed homemade weapons, any kind of threat was taken seriously.

Carlos was the kind of young man I wish I'd had a chance to raise because I could have spared him a lot of pain. But I didn't have that 24–7 influence over him. As time went on at Mid-Valley, I thought the gang influence over him was winning out and believed I had to tighten up my discipline just to keep him in line. He never broke the dress or clean-speech code and his attendance was perfect, as was his general behavior in class. I would talk with him about the need to stand up for what's right, to be a good man and have moral values. In his heart, I believe he wanted that. But his problem stemmed from more than appearance. I discovered it wasn't what he did with me so much as what he stirred up as the de facto leader of all his fellow gang members in that class.

Outside the school, the city streets were crazier than ever in the late nineties. The gang battles for supremacy raged, and the pressure was on Carlos to lead criminal activity. Finally, he was arrested and charged with one felony too many and he appeared headed to the youth prison system. While preparing Carlos's case for court, his probation officer asked me for a statement substantiating some of the charges. Despite my affection for Carlos and the progress he'd made in rehabbing himself, I wrote a letter for the court that was used to justify convicting him. The year in prison eventually stretched to three years because of his fighting and other infractions while imprisoned.

During the time he was in the custody of the California Youth Authority, Carlos wrote to me a few times. He now had time to think, and he said how he appreciated what I'd tried to teach him and regretted any trouble he'd made. He also said how much he regretted involvement in the gang life. I included his letters in a classroom bulletin board display to try and prevent my other students from making the same mistakes. I wrote back to Carlos, giving him all the encouragement I could, and even sent him money on his canteen account so he could have at least a few extra candy bars or cups of noodles to help the time pass more quickly.

Carlos appeared to have struck out at Mid-Valley, yet I wasn't ready to call him a failure. As I discovered later at West Valley, his redemption just took longer than most.

SPEAK NO EVIL

I tell my students that they must dress and speak appropriately for the situation. They only have to look around to see what people are wearing and how they're speaking. Fast-food places have dress codes, as do offices, nursing homes, even private homes where they might be employed. It's also a matter of getting used to being in different settings, and a simple "please" or "thank-you" in a strange place is an icebreaker that usually produces a friendly response. As for curse words, they know that I don't tolerate them at school and that crude language usually works against you in public.

My message to educators and parents: Enforce a zero-tolerance rule against all disrespectful, vulgar, racist, gang-related speech and written expression. Generally, warn kids first if they swear, then suspend them if they continue with offensive language. For example, disrespectful speech toward women, staff, gay or perceived-to-be-gay adults, and students should prompt a warning first and then a suspension. If several repeated suspensions don't cure the problem with a particular student, then he or she needs to be dropped, transferred, or expelled. No law anywhere requires that schools or parents must put up with this kind of denigrating language. I have gone into schools where filthy speech was as common as breathing, and yet within forty-eight hours profanity and ugly talk about any group of people was eliminated from the school. I've found that when schools and parents withdraw their tolerance for abusive verbal behavior, it stops.

Kids talk and act the way they do for only one reason: Their parents and educators allow it. Yet our children are not in the least to blame for this problem. They are only doing what kids have always done. They test their limits. The solution obviously points to setting firm boundaries. Speaking politely, speaking well, speaking without profanity are easy enough principles for my students to accept and try to learn. It's the deeper, culturally learned attitudes that take time and vigilance to reverse or silence. "You can think hurtful or hateful thoughts," I remind them, "but if you speak them, you're going to be held responsible."

Actually, foul language prompted me to get into teaching as a career in the first place. I was working at an outdoor site pouring concrete in Vallejo. It was 1981 and I'd been out in the sun for most of the day and welcomed the afternoon breeze coming off San Francisco Bay. I'd been checking the work my crew had done when I saw three junior high girls walk by me smoking cigarettes. After the smoke cleared, I blurted out after them, "Hey, girls, those things aren't very good for you."

Instantly they whirled around and called me every obscene name I'd ever heard. I wondered, what kind of homes and schools would tolerate that kind of vulgar language every day. That experience echoed my dealings with many members of my own work crew, a handful of friends and acquaintances who subcontracted their labor to me. Although most of them had good hearts and were hard workers, many seemed to be content with a level of thinking and talking that seldom rose above coarse ideas and base expressions. Over a period of time my business grew. I had to hire outside my circle of friends, and drug abuse and theft on the job became intolerable problems.

In short order I left my lucrative concrete business to teach at Cave Elementary because I wanted to make a difference in the lives of young people, not just to straighten out their language but to affect the values that guide their behavior. That was in 1981. Years later, at West Valley, my motives are still the same and certain students with big mouths present the same challenges. One such student was Marla.

MARLA CLEANS UP HER SPEECH

Marla was not a kid from the rough and poor neighborhoods where most of my students lived. The family's ability to rent a house actually made them relatively affluent, though no less dysfunctional than those families of my poorer students.

Marla's way of dealing with her family and personal issues was typical: she used vulgar language and cutting sarcasm to hide her anger and inability to straighten out her life.

Marla shared many examples of these home problems with students and school staff. One story she told was about a birthday party she and her older sister threw for their mother. I had loaned them tables and chairs from the school, even hauled them over to her house in my pickup truck.

On the Monday after the weekend party, when I asked her how it had gone, Marla spit out a few expletives, then apologized for the outburst. She explained that her tipsy mother ended up dancing suggestively with one of her fellow students. I looked at the boy in class as she described her mother's suggestive motions, and he raised his arms and gave me a what-could-I-do expression. Despite Marla's embarrassment during the party, she said her mother didn't see what all the fuss was about. Her mother, she said, was "surprised and disgusted" that Marla and her sister thought there was anything but innocent fun in dancing with the sixteen-year-old boy.

"Marla," I told her. "You did the right thing in objecting to the dance. But when you're talking about it, watch the mouth."

"Sorry, Mr. White."

"You'll learn. It'll become a habit."

Marla did learn, and cleaning up her speech was only the beginning.

Schools

- Enforce a zero-tolerance rule against all disrespectful, vulgar, racist, and gang-related speech and written expression.
- Do the same for gang-related behavior.

Parents

- Tell your teenagers to dress in public as if they were applying for jobs—neat and presentable. No gangster clothes, and the girls shouldn't look like sluts.
- Swearing in any form is out. Cursing creates a crude environment and encourages disrespect toward authority and a moral looseness in all other areas as well. This also applies to parents.
- Rule out sarcasm and hurtful or hateful language.

Rule #3

WE WORK

My mom found this school and I started going here two months ago. I've been sober ever since. I got a job at Wendy's, I'm taking a fashion design class, and I'm working on getting my driver's permit. Things still aren't perfect, but I know I'm on the right path.

—Julie, 16, West Valley student;
former crystal meth addict and dropout

I tell my students that we work because something or someone motivates us to work. Usually, work is a necessity—to earn money to buy things and pay the bills. Yet some people work for the sheer pleasure of the work; they love what they do. And still others work for free, donating their efforts out of duty, kindness, or compassion. Whatever the reasons, to some degree all people, even teenagers, work for or at something. "Not busy work," I explain. "I mean working with a purpose or goal in mind. At your age you should be working *toward* something."

If nothing else, their goal should be to earn and save money while developing steady work habits. Within their first two weeks at West Valley, I require students 16 and over to find part-time jobs that will employ them up to fifteen hours a week. I used to find the jobs for new students, but now I believe they gain real-world experience by hunting for work themselves. Our probation officer, Larry Rothstein, and I prep them for job interviews and they practice filling out application forms for different companies. But all praise for the triumph of landing a job, usually their first ever, belongs to them. If they can't find a job within the two-week deadline, then they don't return to school until they do. We stay in touch so we know where they've applied and how they're doing. Larry and I also pass on tips about who might be hiring.

Like all my rules, the two-week deadline for finding a job puts the burden of keeping to the rule squarely on them. "Try harder," I tell them. I explain that when you are breaking up concrete you might bash the surface fifty times and not crack it. You assume your effort has been for nothing. But you swing the sledgehammer one more time and that's when the cement cracks and falls apart. Succeeding at anything often takes that extra bit of effort. One more step, one more job interview, one more swing with the sledgehammer. This is why we at West Valley call ourselves "the Sledgehammers."

Having a driver's license helps the older students become independent. If they or their families can't cover the cost of a driver's education class, I'll pay for them to take it, often aided by a wonderfully supportive local foundation. Some students eventually earn and save enough money to buy their own cars. Though most of the kids land entry-level jobs at fast-food restaurants, ice cream parlors, and retail stores of all kinds, some jobs require employees to drive. Larry and I also help them set up "job shadows," which means being with a professional for a half day. Following around a sheriff's deputy or TV journalist often whets their appetites for different careers—and shows them the importance of driving in certain jobs.

As for our thirteen-to-fifteen-year-old students, if they can't find a job, they're required to do at least three weekdays a week of voluntary community service. This can include one or more of a range of activities, including helping people or animals at convalescent homes and pet shelters, singing in a church choir, or attending court-ordered counseling sessions on anger management. Larry verifies their attendance or participation by having the kids bring him notes from their counselors or activity supervisors on letterhead.

All students, no matter what their age, must also take and pass at least one class per semester at a nearby community college or vocational school. Navigating a college campus and registration process can be frightening for a thirteen-year-old, but I tell them to approach it as an adventure. As with jobs, we offer whatever backup support is needed for them to succeed. Once they settle into a class and in many cases hold their own with students who are eighteen, nineteen, and much older, they return with an expanded view of the world and their own future potential. Whether it's learning sign language, taking college algebra, or writing papers for a Business 101 class, they gain some sophistication as well as college credits. More important, their expanding self-image boosts their confidence and improves their bearing.

WORK BUILDS CONFIDENCE

Working and being paid generally build confidence in anyone with low self-esteem. My students are especially transformed when the adult working world takes them seriously. Nola, for example, the student with the Tinker Bell and Raiders necklaces, completely changed in her demeanor once she got a job. Leaving her life of drugs and gangs, the big girl with practically no self-esteem had come to West Valley to give school another try and soon she was thriving in class and on the job. She excelled in her studies and her supervisor raved about her diligence and sensitivity in dealing with customers.

Nola loved everything about West Valley and our program appeared to fit her perfectly. She even welcomed my rule about staying clean and sober because the voluntary drug screening helped keep her off drugs. With a clear mind she focused on her academic studies as well as her new part-time job as a restaurant waitress and cashier.

But with any transformation as extreme as Nola's, challenges invariably arise. Her studies and after-school job suddenly demanded all her time. Also, the stress of making such a radical change in her daily habits sometimes triggered her anger at other female students. These situations were always peacefully resolved, until finally her temper was under control. But Nola's effort to maintain a drug- and gang-free lifestyle came under attack from her father. Nola told me her dad and the local gang members were smoking so much marijuana in her home that she feared she would test dirty through a "contact high" and get thrown out of West Valley. She said she had begged her dad to stop but he ignored her.

As she told me this, she broke down, sobbing. I immediately called her dad and demanded that he come in for a conference at eight the next morning. We met in the shadow of the school's parking lot dumpster (my "office," as it's known, because I have so many impromptu student and parent meetings there). As I ranted, accused, and pleaded with her dad to just once try to be a real father and quit ruining Nola's life, I looked up and saw the face of lifelong regret. In the sunlight his haggard, prematurely aged face showed the effects of a life of drug abuse, hard physical labor, poor health, and poverty. Finally, Nola's father, an illiterate, tearful, ill man, closed his eyes and said, "I'm sorry, teacher. I promise you, no more *drogas en mi casa*. I love my daughter and I will do this for her." He kept his word and Nola stayed on course with her plan to study, work, and maybe someday have a career.

JOB BENEFITS

Requiring my students to have jobs that they find on their own removes the family from the equation. The kids are the ones who apply for jobs. They're the ones filling out the job applications, sweating the interviews, taking the tests. They're the ones who are hired. It's solely their achievement; Mom and Dad have nothing to do with it.

Other responsible adults obviously are convinced that these teenagers can make money for their businesses, that they're worth hiring on their own merits. This brings these boys and girls instant validation. They've crossed over into another world, one with time clocks, duties, and expectations. For the first time in their lives they're being treated as trustworthy, responsible adults themselves.

Their jobs, moreover, don't interfere with their school work because we closely monitor both and make adjustments when problems arise. Studies show that students who work fifteen to twenty hours per week academically outperform both the students without jobs as well as those who work more than twenty hours per week. Like all things with children, quick fixes are scarce. Where paid work is concerned, you don't just stick them in a fast-food place or behind a department store cash register and then forget about them. If you do, the next thing you know, the manager is scheduling them for a forty-hour week and having them close the restaurant after midnight. The next day they're falling asleep on you in class and learning nothing.

To make the employment an experience that contributes to rather than detracts from their schooling, we keep regular tabs on their schedules and their relationships with their managers and coworkers. Typical issues are: making sure they're getting paid for the hours they work; checking with their managers to see how our students can get promoted to positions of greater responsibility; and ironing out problems (such as working too slowly or being rude with customers) and then trying to train the student at school how to improve in those areas. For example, a local company that sold diet supplement drinks initially hired one of our fourteen-year-old female students just to answer the phone. We kept in regular communication with the company owner, encouraging him to challenge this talented young lady with greater responsibility. Seeing that she was very capable and computer literate, the owner ultimately moved her into another department, where she was handling most of the shipping and receiving paperwork for the $8 million worth of business that his company did annually. Because of the way we constantly coach our students and because of our primary emphasis on attitude and honest, hardworking behavior, many of our students end up in managerial and supervisory roles at the companies employing them.

Working regularly for money often changes the lives of teenagers who previously wasted much of their time in unproductive, often destructive, activities. Suddenly, mandatory school attendance means there's little or no time for just hanging out with friends, doing drugs, drinking beer, or having sex. In fact, statistics prove that the best birth control method among teenagers is having a job and doing well in school.

GIRLS ARE THE KEY

I discovered the connection between pregnancies and school-work activities after I began to require that my students all have part-time jobs. Before this rule was in effect, pregnancies among my students were commonplace and were hardly ever surprising, no matter how much I warned them about the consequences of early sex. After I began requiring that they work at least fifteen hours a week and push themselves academically, pregnancies virtually disappeared.

In Nola's case, school and job duties replaced the time she used to spend being promiscuous with the gang crowd before she came to West Valley. As she said during a class discussion about sex, "I'm so busy with work, I don't have time for that. Even if I wanted to, there's just no time."

Nola and most of the girls in class agreed that a full schedule of school, work, future career activities, and daily adult supervision is the best birth control method. This is because teenage girls have a craving, but it's not for sexual intercourse with uncommitted, dead-end thugs. Girls definitely have a craving for a daily life that is interesting, productive, and challenging, and leaves them with feelings of hope and self-worth. Truant teenage girls give in to promiscuity when they have too many unsupervised hours to kill day and night, lack money and moral guidance, and follow friends into regular drug and alcohol use. Almost inevitably, this leads to meaningless sex, shallow relationships with different boys, and the nightmarish effects of AIDS and other sexually transmitted diseases.

One healthy side effect of requiring students to have full schedules is that our girls tend to rekindle previous relationships with female friends, get out of bad relationships with boyfriends more quickly, start to enjoy group dates, and connect with better boys. Their new relationships usually are not rife with overemotional commitment, dramatics, and abuse.

Since starting West Valley Leadership Academy in 2000 with

Bob McGill—my teaching partner at Mid-Valley, who now runs a teen mom program in our building—many of our past students have gone on to be law abiding and gainfully employed as computer programmers, electricians, medical technicians, mechanics, restaurant managers—you name it. From what they tell me, our program affected for the better even many of those I dropped or who dropped out. By following my tighter rules, they managed to turn themselves away from the pitfalls of drug and alcohol abuse, idleness, crime, even premarital parenthood. Almost all have stayed out of prison and avoided early, violent deaths, and now live free of domestic abuse.

I'm convinced that the girls in the program deserve much of the credit for these successes. Having as many as we've had at West Valley is a statistical aberration because alternative schools for problem kids generally are so out of control that girls choose not to attend them. The boys are too lewd and too aggressive in their behaviors. Yet from the beginning Bob and I believed that girls were the key to turning the kids around on the main issues: sexual promiscuity, lying, profanity, disrespecting people and property, and an ignorance of compassion for those in need.

Requiring all students to have part-time jobs and stay in other after-school activities helped halt the pregnancies. But the underlying truth for many of our girls is that they've grown up abused and submissive to the males in their families. When they reach adolescence, they're handed over to boyfriends who continue the same treatment, and the results are often made worse by the girls' self-abuse. The girls start to believe that they're next to worthless, that they're good for only one thing: having babies by one thug after another.

Rhonda, our first girl to graduate from West Valley, shone from the first moment she walked into class. As usual, Larry had completed the intake interview and she had already heard his intro talk. So when she entered she knew more about me as a teacher than I knew about her as a student or her days as a delinquent. Rhonda, an African American fifteen years of age, had a smile that lit up a room; her eyes sparkled as much as her big hoop earrings. As soon as class lessons began she participated as if she were a longtime student, repeatedly shooting her hand up to answer questions or add her two cents' worth to the discussion.

I usually avoid directing any questions to new students, preferring to let them join in when they feel comfortable, to allow them a chance to check out how we do things at West Valley. Since Rhonda needed no prompting and was quite open about why she came to us, I found out that she came from a large family and one of her older brothers had been one of our first graduates. Unlike her brother, who'd had issues with drugs and the gang life, Rhonda's main handicap was her near inability to stay out of fights and screaming arguments with other girls. Her brother had managed to straighten out his life with us and had received his diploma, and I expected nothing less from her.

"I'm here because my mom brought me," she said when I asked her what led her to West Valley. She noted that she had barely attended the local high school, "but I think I'm going to like it here."

Rhonda predicted her own success by volunteering to do anything I brought up as an activity. She was always game. If a job was available, she'd interview and get it. If a class assignment was due within the hour, she'd work the hardest and finish first. If I held a contest in the form of a pop quiz, she'd win it. When we formed a school choir, she'd not only lead the singing but also write her own song and perform it solo and unaccompanied. And when visitors needed a tour of the school, Rhonda would jump at the chance to guide them around. By the end of her presentation, the visitors practically wanted to adopt her.

By all measures, Rhonda was an immediate and spectacular success in and out of class. Aside from her smarts, bubbly enthusiasm, and an innate strong work ethic, it seemed to me that her finest quality was her motivation. She had an abundance of self-starting ideas and projects in mind. However, some students' strength can ebb and flow as their confidence level rises and drops. Ironically, as I show later, Rhonda's motivation slowed despite a string of amazing job triumphs.

TEACHING THE WORK ETHIC

Unlike Rhonda, if kids don't have a work ethic when they come to me, their new jobs help them develop one. This involves their grooming, punctuality, and ability to interact effectively with all kinds of people. I've found that the discipline they practice on the job also spills over to school. Those who work part-time do better in school. Also, West Valley rules about showing up, dressing and speaking right, telling the truth, and respecting other people are all reinforced in the workplace. If they didn't know it before, they quickly learn how they're expected to appear and behave. And if they cheat or skip work, there are serious consequences, which is what happens at West Valley when they slip up. I prepare them with real-world rules, unlike most public schools, where rule breakers often face pathetically weak consequences.

Once teenagers are hired and working, paychecks may be thrilling to receive, but they, too, come with obligations attached, starting with a budget of expenses. First, we require students to deposit 25 percent of their income in bank savings accounts. We suggest that half of the rest be given to their families to help out with home expenses, and that they keep the remainder for their own use. Every pay period, they must show Larry their paycheck stubs and savings deposit slips. To get them used to handling their own finances, we have class lessons about personal finances, interest earnings, credit, inflation, investments, and the stock market. They even learn to play the market in class by tracking and buying allotted shares of stock with theoretical amounts of money. I break them into teams and they research prospective companies on the Web to find out whether certain stocks are worth buying.

MY MOM TEACHES ME A LESSON

With these assignments, as with everything they do, I remind them of the satisfaction in doing a job well. In repetitive activities it's normal for anyone to fall into a work-is-drudgery attitude. I was lucky enough to have someone at home actually demonstrate pleasure in doing simple tasks well, and I tell the story to my students.

To my nine-year-old eyes, my mother might as well have been performing a circus trick—it was that unusual. It was the start of a new school year and my family wanted to take a vacation that summer, but money was short. My mom and dad figured that if my sister and I helped them clean the house each week, they'd eliminate the need for a cleaning lady and we'd be able to save enough money to go camping. My particular job was to scrub all the floors in the house each week.

But first my mother had to teach me. She filled a bucket with soapy water, knelt down, and with a hand brush showed me how to scrub and rinse the linoleum one section at a time. I remember they were large sections, about four feet across. After she finished scrubbing a section, she'd wipe it dry with a cloth, polish it with another cloth, and finish the whole process by running her hand over the gleaming, yellowish surface. She smiled and then said, "Doesn't that floor feel clean!"

I took in the gleam and then stared at my mother for a moment. I didn't get it. "Mom," I cried, "what are you, nuts? Do you really like cleaning a floor?"

She turned to me and calmly said, "Well, Paul, I don't like it the way I like eating ice cream. But it's a different kind of like. There's just a satisfaction in doing a hard job well."

I looked down at the floor and did see a difference between clean and shiny and dull and dirty. Reluctantly I nodded, and she handed me the brush. I knelt down beside the bucket of soapy water and began to imitate what she had done—the same deliberate, circular strokes, the same rinsing, the same drying and polishing. Now and then I'd sit back and admire the part I'd finished, then continue, focusing on every stroke, getting into a rhythm I liked.

For a few Fridays after that first time, my friends would come over to watch me scrub the kitchen floor. I got to like seeing it come out all clean and polished. I also felt like Tom Sawyer because my buddies saw how I liked what I was doing. They wanted to get down and scrub the floor, too. They begged me, "Let me do one! Is this how? Can I try?" I'd sit back and let them take turns, happily supervising their work.

From what I can see, many Americans have gotten away from the act of rolling up their sleeves and taking satisfaction in doing simple work well. Maybe we think it's beneath us, that we're educated and above such things, or that menial labor is for someone else. Whatever the case, children still have to learn the simplest of chores by example and in small ways, either at home or in school. I tell my kids that if something's broken, you fix it. If something spills, you clean it up. If something's done wrong, you do it over. If a brother or sister is struggling, you help them. And if you don't know how to do something, ask somebody who does.

I was lucky. My mother's floor-scrubbing lesson came relatively early in my childhood and helped define my own work ethic. Most of my students never had such lessons or examples in their homes. I learned to savor the satisfactions and compliments of doing my chores well, but my parents also held me accountable for things I did wrong or just skipped altogether. Home or school, it didn't matter. If I sassed a teacher, they'd hear about it and come down on me hard and fast. There were no days of pausing to think about it. And they never would have accepted an excuse that the teacher was picking on me. If I didn't straighten out my room when I said I would, one of them would be on me in seconds. I didn't like getting caught and having to pay the price of a scolding or some privilege denied. Only years later did I realize my parents loved me enough to make me do the right thing.

By contrast, most of my students have never been watched at home the way I was. Most of their parents, who are frequently single moms, don't seem to care or are so weighed down by their own jobs and emotional needs that they just want peace at home and not endless fights with their kids. So kids learn their work habits amid the disorder and chaos at home, taking their cues from available adults and friends and whatever they can cull from their TV, film, and music idols.

FINDING THE RIGHT MOTIVATION

Teachers everywhere face the tough work of motivating bored, restless, or disruptive students. We all have our favorite ways of trying to move students to act on their own. When my father and school pals scoffed at my early basketball skills, that was incentive enough to turn me into a hoop-practicing fiend, perfecting moves that earned me a starting spot on the high school varsity team and a college scholarship. As a teacher, I accent the positive in student class work, but I'm forever trying to find the right self-motivation button to push at the right time.

On my first stint as a long-term substitute teacher at Cave Elementary, one lethargic sixth-grader defied all my efforts to push him to improve his spelling. He'd failed every spelling test I'd ever given him and was the worst speller in a class of notoriously poor spellers. Finally, I came up with a challenge for him that involved the other students. I told him that if he passed the next day's spelling test, I would buy pizza for the whole class. But if he failed, there would be no pizza. He thought this over and flatly said, "I'll do it."

"You'll take the test?"

"I'll pass it."

The next day he sat directly in front of me. When the class took the test, I watched him closely. He took his time to finish. Just before our lunch break I corrected the tests. When I announced that he had received an A-minus, everybody exploded in whoops and cheers, gathering around his desk to congratulate him. I ordered the pizzas and we enjoyed them. Later, when the last bell rang, the kids eagerly headed for the door to go home. My new spelling whiz was one of the last to leave the room, carrying with him a paper bag with something long and narrow inside. "What's in the bag?" I asked him.

"A little baseball bat."

"What for?"

"If I'd failed," he explained, "there'd have been no pizza, Mr. White, and I'd have had a hard time getting home. They'd all have been after me."

During the rest of the school year, this same boy failed every spelling test he took. I could never again stir him to pass the test. But on that one occasion I managed to push the right button at the right time, proving that his lack of proficiency (and many of the other students') was not due to aptitude but attitude. The night before the test he must have worked overtime memorizing words, obsessed with his mission. Although I don't endorse his baseball bat solution, it proved to me that motivation is everything in teaching students effectively.

FINDING A JOB

At the other end of the motivation scale is a boy who came to West Valley eager to change his life but unfortunately saddled with years of truancy, fighting gangbangers, hanging with his homies, and a serious dependence on pot. In Larry's standard two-and-a-half-hour enrollment session with this boy and his mom, he meticulously explained the school rules, repeating such phrases as "show up on time," "clean and sober," and "tell the truth." They were told the rules, but apparently the new boy thought they were flexible. His life so far had been filled with third and fourth chances and a lot of responsible folks looking the other way.

Not surprisingly, he arrived five minutes late to school the first day. I repeated the rule about coming to school on time. "The bus was late," he said.

"You should have taken an earlier one," I said. "See you tomorrow . . . on time."

He looked stunned as I showed him to the front door. The next day he arrived about half an hour early—and of course he was never again late.

The second rule he violated was failing to stay clean and sober. Right away he offered to have his urine tested—it's a voluntary procedure. He tested dirty, but promised he'd test clean the next time. A week later he tested dirty again. I dropped him until he could tell me he was clean and sober. Another week passed and he called to say he was ready to return. He asked me to test him. I did, and he passed.

His next hurdle was finding a job within two weeks. He'd never worked before, hadn't ever applied for jobs, and was slow to pound away at it. Two weeks passed and he was still empty-handed. Once again I had to drop him until he found something. He knew what he had to do, and every day he'd call me to report his job-hunting progress. I could tell he was actually *working* at looking for work. I couldn't interfere because I believed he had to get hired by himself. Finally, one day he called me during class to say proudly he'd found a job. Could he come back?

"You bet," I said. "We're waiting for you."

When I announced the news, his new classmates cheered.

A sixteen-year-old pothead with no work experience, this student had come to West Valley *wanting* to change. That's the part I can't give them. It has to come from them. I can give them the commonsense reasons, but at bottom they have to have it somewhere in themselves to want to turn things around, to want to leave the weed and booze, to want to stop dead-end pursuits, to want to learn, to want to work for money.

Schools

- Encourage students to find paid part-time employment.

Parents

- Push part-time work for your kids, but monitor it consistently to make sure it remains a positive experience. They can earn money, stay out of trouble, learn practical work habits, and in many cases learn about proper dress and behavior in the workplace.

Rule #4

WE TELL THE TRUTH

[Mr. White] trusted me enough to run a little store in the school. I'd sell soups, chips, soda, and candy to students. He'd pay me at the end of the week. It wasn't much but it taught me to be honest and not steal money.

—Corey, 22, county worker; former West Valley student; former drug addict and gang member

Tell the truth, I tell my students; if you're doing something you've got to lie about, change what you're doing. *Don't lie.* When I say this, the new kids, even some of the regulars, usually look at me as if I'm asking the impossible. I try to make it sound as easy as a reflex: You just don't lie. Honesty is the absolute foundation of everything we do at West Valley. If you're not living honestly, trust dies and relationships fall apart—and it's not because the issues are unsolvable. It's because you lie about them so much that they get out of control. Lying little or lying big—it doesn't matter which—becomes a habit that sooner or later is destructive.

Los Angeles County has dozens of schools like ours for high-risk kids. Yet West Valley is virtually the only one that doesn't do pat-downs and metal-detecting searches every morning as students enter the building. We've been incident free and safe since the day we opened our doors in 2000 because honesty, not metal detection, is the key to our security system. We have an honest relationship with our students, encourage an esprit de corps based on moral courage, and integrity, and expect them to respect our policies and reputation. When it comes to academics, we use this foundation of honesty to teach that an honest F is better than a dishonest A, that it's what you're learning that counts, and that how you go about achieving something is more important than what you achieve.

When we discuss drugs and alcohol, I use my personal example. From my own days of minimal marijuana smoking in college, I tell the students that I never said I was going to quit; I only vowed to stop lying. I never used drugs again because I couldn't use them without lying to almost everyone in my life.

"Right," we teach, is not what you get away with, and "wrong" is not what you get caught doing. I tell my kids that there *are* moral absolutes and standards. Life works better and you feel better about yourself when you're living "right" and "owning your stuff"—taking responsibility for what you do—than when you're sneaking around. I'm more tolerant with a student who loses his temper and kicks over a chair than I am with a child who repeatedly tries to sneak in gum or a cell phone during the day, and then lies about having it when I call him on it. The once-in-a-blue-moon chair kick is an extreme, impulsive reaction of a kind that is not so unusual for teens who are learning how to control their emotions. Persistently sneaking in gum or a cell phone, on the other hand, springs from a more calculating kind of amoral behavior, the kind that also leads to turning a blind eye when any other person does something illegal or immoral.

In implementing our honesty-based security system, we also use the method perfected by El Al, the Israeli airline. El Al's record for security is exceptionally good, and yet they do far fewer searches of passengers than other major airlines. Their representatives focus on making personal contact with the passengers standing in line, looking them in the eye, talking to them about their travel plans, watching their body language, and just getting a gut feeling for their character and honesty. In the same way, every morning, when our students come into the school, I greet them, shake hands, and ask them how everything's going, mentally comparing their behavior with baseline normal behavior. I call this my "rounds." When something has changed in their lives or attitude, I can usually spot it and deal with it while it's a small problem.

Newcomers to West Valley are always impressed with the clean and pristine look of the place: there is no grime, no graffiti, and there are no metal detectors or sensor systems. Weapons of any kind, of course, are forbidden on campus, and unless students receive permission they're also forbidden to bring to school cell phones, radios, pagers, CD players, and other distracting electronic devices. If a banned item is found and no one claims it, everyone sits in silence until the owner speaks up and gives me the truth.

Periodically, I remind them of what they cannot stick in their pockets. Maybe three times in the past six years I've had to pat down students I suspected were concealing weapons. For me and for students, because such searches are so rare, safety inside the school is a given. We know that we are in a safe, nonviolent place. Apart from a single security guard assigned to watch the exterior of the building and locked outside doors that open with key codes, our only security system is straightforward truth and trust.

I encourage absolute candor with my students. What we say to each other may not always be what we like to hear, but it's going to be the truth. I tell them that I once ran a business doing deals on a handshake, and I never got burned. Both sides trusted the other to be honest and we all wanted others to trust us as good men and women. Ultimately, that's all we have. When I look for this level of trust in the kids—actually, *insist* that there be a desire to be trustworthy—invariably I find the good persons inside. If there's a problem of conscience or questionable behavior, I go right at him or her, looking for the good, truthful person inside. I don't just let things take their course, which is how most people treat teenagers. The passive, wait-and-see approach only leads to temporary fixes and ultimately kids spiral out of control.

GETTING MY SOUL BACK

"So, Mr. White, you ever lie?" The question comes from Frankie, the former fringe gangster and pot smoker who got the cheers when he landed his first job. He sits at the end of one of the tables in the second row of students, next to a wall map of the world.

"Oh, big time," I answer. I then describe how, earlier, my drug use eventually led to a moral crisis of conscience. During my sophomore and junior years in college I was smoking pot a few times a week. I hid what I was doing from those I thought would disapprove—my parents and steady girlfriend at the time—and I gave them no reason to ask if I smoked pot. Though no one ever spoke to me about drug use and how a drug conviction limits job prospects, I knew my habit was illegal and wrong. That's why I hid it, and I probably would have lied about it if asked. What gnawed at me was lying to myself. I kept thinking I wasn't hurting anyone, that it was no big deal. What's the harm in a little weed now and then? But I was fooling myself. It *was* a big deal. Otherwise, it wouldn't have eaten away at me. I was losing all self-respect and feeling morally weak. Finally, I was so disgusted with myself for lying that I quit.

"They ever catch you?" Frankie asks.

"No," I answer, but add that if I had been caught and convicted, it might have interfered with my getting a teaching credential.

I gaze around at my students, most of them former druggies. "The day I stopped lying to myself was the day I stopped using," I say. "That was more than thirty years ago and I've been clean and sober ever since. When I started smoking pot, like a lot of you, I didn't know how much I was risking—and I don't mean lost jobs and opportunities. I mean loss of self-respect, feeling you have no moral courage, no integrity. That was the price I paid for lying. Once I stopped lying, it was like getting my soul back. Big relief."

I've told my drug-days story many times in class, not so much because I want my students to know I lied and had a habit but because I myself don't want to forget the time in my life when I was weak and unprincipled and had no controls on my behavior. I didn't like what I was doing and was ashamed of myself. The kids understand this because they're trying to leave behind a few bad habits, too. My frankness in speaking of my own moral failings helps me connect with them. When I open up, they trust me to understand their problems and they also open up. I encourage parents and teachers to honestly disclose similar conflicts of conscience in their lives, even though they may not think it's useful. If adults don't open up, they're likely to be seen as hypocrites by children.

Living an honest life is a struggle, but my students are succeeding. For the first time in years they're coming to class every day, they're off drugs, and they actually *like* what they're becoming. It's a new feeling and takes adjusting to, but I tell them it's like coming out into sudden sunshine. You have to squint for a while until you get used to the light. I also tell them that there's no need to lie now, not if they're following the rules: showing up, dressing and speaking right, staying clean and sober, respecting others, practicing compassion, studying, and working.

Admittedly, many of my students have larger issues in their past than the marijuana and deception in mine. Some have done very awful things, but I don't fault just them. I blame their parents and schools for allowing them to become the holy terrors they were. Together, parents and teachers failed to give these kids a template for moral values, for distinguishing right from wrong, especially for learning about the consequences of lying. I remind my students that lying starts just by being human. Even the most humble of us is proud. We have names, identities, and personalities. We protect these with some degree of self-delusion or self-deception by presenting massaged, inflated views of ourselves. And without frequent, sometimes harsh, reality checks, we tend to go on believing our distortions. If we're not called on it, we can even justify a life of lies.

LIES GO ONLY SO FAR

After he settled into his job, Frankie amazed me and his more experienced classmates by how quick and complete his turnaround was. He tested clean for drugs, he was sober, and he hadn't missed a class since his first day at school, when I sent him home for arriving a few minutes late. He was also attending an auto mechanics class at the local vocational school. Proudly beaming, he even announced to me after class that his morals were on track because he was back to regularly attending church twice a week with his mother and sisters. This should have raised a red flag in my mind. But at the time I thought such an admission fell in line with all the other positive aspects of his life.

What finally brought Frankie down were his lies, or, to put it another way, his failure to tell the truth. Mainly, he was not telling me what was in his heart. Almost by accident I found out that he had been keeping up his gang connections. I saw an

Internet-posted photograph of him gang-posturing with another boy who was making a gang sign with his hands, all while on a West Valley school field trip. He had disrespected our program, and I felt betrayed and confronted him. Frankie shrugged off what he'd done as a minor misstep on school time, professed to still being down with his homies, and casually accepted being dropped from school as the price he had to pay to keep his gang identity.

It pained me to see him toss away a chance to educate himself in a drug-free environment just to return to his old habits. On the surface, he wanted me to believe he'd left the gang culture and dropped all apparent signs of participation in that life. All along, however, just under the surface, he still clung to hardcore *vida loca* values. When I met with Frankie's mother about dropping him, she was defiant and hateful. Never once did she blame her son for anything, despite clear evidence that he had never left his gang. She showed no regret for his behavior nor did she express any appreciation for what we'd done for him. This kind of misguided parental support almost ensures that Frankie's problems will get worse.

A few days after he left the school he dropped by to pick up his transcripts so he could transfer to another school. He might have chosen to apologize for betraying our trust in him. Instead, he appeared wearing his best gang shirt, a Raiders jersey. Taciturn and sullen, he picked up his papers and left the building. I heard later that he had given up his auto mechanics class and had returned to some of his old ways. After such a promising start, I could only believe that Frankie's future was now back on the ropes.

For all the deceptive Frankies I've had as students, there have been many who stood up for the rules with utmost respect, even if their confessions of breaking them got them dropped from school. I remember one boy, an ex–crack addict, who took to the program for several months and then began behaving erratically in class. He appeared hyper and jumpy, one knee continually bouncing under the table. I needed to test him, so I asked if I could run our usual urinalysis test. He could have refused, but if he had, I would have known he was probably violating the clean-and-sober rule. He said I could test him.

Such a test, which I pay for because my school district does not require drug testing, takes a matter of minutes to run; one simply immerses a disposable dipstick in an inch of urine. "Will the test be dirty?" I asked.

Without hesitating, he said, "Yes, I'm using." He could easily have said, "No," taken the test, and then claimed that some cold medicine he'd been taking had messed up the results. But he didn't.

"You know the rule," I said. "You can't stay."

He thanked me for admitting him to the program in the first place, then walked out of the building in tears. Two years later, he called me. I hadn't seen him since he left the school. "Mr. White," he said, "I just wanted to thank you for kicking me out of West Valley."

He went on to say that my dropping him had prompted a revelation. It caused him to confront his crack habit and realize he didn't want to remain an addict. So he stopped completely. He then returned to the high school he'd been enrolled in before but had rarely attended. This time he finished and received a diploma. He also kept the McDonald's job he'd gotten when he was at West Valley and became a top employee. He's now halfway through a college program to be a medical records technician. By doing his best to live honestly, he created an integrity in himself that inevitably carried over into his studies and work.

LIES AND CONSEQUENCES

Most of my students come to me as chronic liars. I tell them I don't care how or why they learned to lie, deceive, and con themselves and others. In children, lying can be common for all kinds of reasons—they seek dares and thrills and they've never been caught, or if they have, they've never been seriously punished. But just as kids can learn to be dishonest, they can learn to be honest. They can learn to live by the truth, which at West Valley they can see is not impossible.

I also tell them it's usually hard to admit to a lie, to apologize, to face embarrassment, anger, hurt looks, even punishment. But if we don't own up to the lie, tiny as it may be, we go on lying, covering up, pretending, and deceiving. "It's like getting caught stealing money out of your mother's purse," I say during a discussion of embezzlement and personal finances. "What's happening?"

A hand goes up in the back row and the bright-eyed kid says, "You get busted."

"Right."

"What if it's worth it?"

"Well," I say, "that's up to you. Either you steal it or you don't. But if you do, you might have to face the consequences."

"I guess I don't."

"You *guess?*"

"Okay, no guessing."

"You bet there's no guessing."

We laugh, and before returning to our discussion, I tell them about the time when I didn't get caught stealing and where that led. As a fifth-grader growing up in a white suburb of Detroit, I started hanging around with a boy whose dad was in jail. It was a family in chaos. The boy's mom didn't care what he did and consequently he got to do whatever he wanted, like stealing candy from a neighborhood store. I thought that was a good idea and I started shoplifting, too.

The boy knew my parents and figured they would just about kill me if they knew what I was doing. So he started blackmailing me, ordering me around, making me do his chores, even asking me for money. I became his virtual slave because I was afraid he'd tell my parents, and this hold he had on me was driving me crazy. I didn't know what to do. All I knew was that I hated this kid and what he was doing to me. He practically had me on a leash. "Paul!" he'd shout. "Come here! Give me some of your candy!" If I hesitated, he'd add with a smile, "Or I'll tell your folks what you did."

After a few weeks I couldn't take it anymore. I went to my mother and confessed to stealing candy bars. After scolding me, she took me down to the store to apologize to the store owner. I paid him for the missing candy and he thanked me for being honest. As I walked back home with my mother, she was quiet, probably to let the lesson I had learned about stealing sink in.

The next day, the same boy saw me going to school and yelled, "Hey, Paul! Get over here!" Cool as can be, I walked up to him and told him that I had confessed to my mother and that he didn't have anything on me anymore. I was free!

AMERICA'S FRONT DOOR

The same day we discuss blackmail, I also discuss personal finance. I require each student to save 25 percent of their earnings in a savings account. This is part of their initial agreement with the school. They have to show me a deposit-and-balance record every month, along with the pay stubs from their jobs. Saving money, I tell them, has many uses and like everything they learn at West Valley, it has to become a habit.

"My job is to get you ready," I say. "I don't want to see you in section-8 housing projects. I don't want you in subsidized, two-hundred-dollar-a-month apartments. I don't want you waiting in line for free cheese. I don't want you going to free medical clinics. No, I want you to have medical insurance to pay your own doctor and dentist bills. I want you to go shopping where you want to shop. I want you to be able to walk in America's front door and get whatever you want by paying for it."

To do all this, I tell them, they have to have three things: skills, good work habits, and a sense of values, so they don't get caught up in doing the wrong thing. "But what's the piece that's missing here?" I ask. "What's lacking?"

"Work ethic?" says Nola, the student whose father promised

not to smoke weed around his daughter. One of my best students ever, she is about to graduate, having just completed all her credits.

"Could be," I say. "Actually, you have to watch all three things—*that's* the missing piece. If you're hanging around too much and getting lazy, it's your work ethic. If your computer skills are slipping, you've got to study and practice more to catch up. If you're tempted to do the wrong thing—oops, you've got to watch your values. The wrong thing, by the way, usually involves lying. Read the headlines, listen to the news. Thieves lie, drunks and addicts lie, drug dealers lie, some politicians and CEOs lie, just as cheating husbands and wives lie."

"And cheating boyfriends," Nola interjects, prompting some grins from the boys and eyeball rolling from the girls.

"They get into all kinds of problems," I continue, "because they have to lie."

During my years pouring concrete, I seldom had time for a normal lunch break. Likewise, as a teacher for more than twenty-five years, maybe two times I've had a pleasant, uninterrupted lunch. This is because working with wet concrete and teaching children are similar in at least one way. To get the best results, you may not ignore or neglect what's happening. With my students, I spend that critical, informal time we call lunch break talking with them, listening, observing, and offering any kind of help that is needed. Like setting concrete, kids are active and restless and I must keep a hand on the whole process while shaping and molding. I expect honesty all the time but watch for lies because soon enough they will harden into the shape they're going to be for life.

SEX AND LIES

From what I've seen in my years of teaching and counseling adolescents, the first casualty in teenage sex is truth. The boy usually lies to the girl about his deep devotion to her. The girl lies to herself, trying to believe that the boy really loves her. Both of them lie to their parents about what they're doing and when they're doing it. And finally, parents lie to themselves, too, trying to believe that if they don't think or talk about kids' sex lives, it will go away.

Of course, if everyone told the truth, none of these deceptions would occur. Relationship problems wouldn't exactly disappear overnight but at least with everyone involved openly and honestly, you'd be heading in the right direction to find solutions. As for how schools and parents face sex and sexuality among adolescents, that's determined by the rules and examples we set for children, which guide them as they mature. If the rules are unclear, lax, or nonexistent, nature follows its own course. There are consequences—and *nothing* has the ability to change a child's future more quickly than a pregnancy or a sexually transmitted disease.

"Think about what you're doing," I say, adding that not many sixteen-year-old girls envision a good time as staying home with a baby, cleaning up an apartment, shopping for groceries, and standing in a line at the clinic for the baby's checkups. Their sexual activity should begin at the same time they think they would make a good parent. "No teenager ever died from *not* having sexual intercourse," I tell them. "There are no known deaths from that."

They laugh, but then I go on to describe some of the dangerous diseases they can get without actually having intercourse,
just by "fooling around" with a promiscuous partner. I'll also
describe the grim, heartrending choices kids and their families
have to make after a couple has an unwanted pregnancy. They
must choose to abort or to have an unwanted child who will
most likely grow up in a life of want, abuse, and unfulfilled
dreams. "Think about it," I say. "Neither one of these lousy
choices would have to be made if they hadn't told lies."

In both one-on-one and group discussions of sex, I'm old
school all the way to marriage. I can lecture and advise, I can
show them the statistics, I can scare them with descriptions of
what AIDS does, I can do all this daily, and yet I can't actually
stop them from having sex. If passions take over and the brakes
aren't applied, none of my commonsense arguments are strong
enough to help them save sexual intercourse for their marriage
partner. In my experience, the only consistent way I know of
curbing premarital sex is by instilling in a child a strong belief
in a spiritual law that condemns it.

Many adults believe such an absolute moral standard is unrealistic and unachievable. I don't think it is, considering that
most people follow religious or spiritual laws against murder
and theft. Why can't the sexual standard be taught in religious
homes with the same conviction as the other two laws?

Not all parents, however, are religious or are observant. To
them—and I say this to the parents of my students—I offer the
following list of nos they can impose on their teenagers: no
boyfriend or girlfriend sleep-overs at the other's house; no long
periods together in seclusion; no staying out all night with a

boyfriend or girlfriend; no oral sex, a precursor to intercourse; and, most important, *no lies.*

AFFECTING SEXUAL, DRUG-USE, AND DRINKING BEHAVIOR

The role of the parent and teacher in influencing a child's sexual as well as drug-use and drinking behaviors cannot be overstated. Adults must take the "high ground" in both issues, and must serve as role models by practicing what they preach.

As far as minors having sexual intercourse is concerned, the position of any responsible adult is a no-brainer: it's illegal, it's immoral, it ruins a relationship, and it can greatly harm your children. While teen pregnancy rates have gone up at just about every other school, West Valley's have dropped to almost nothing. One reason is that we strongly emphasize the illegality of intercourse: anyone in California who has intercourse with a minor is committing statutory rape and under any one of many possible scenarios could go to prison and have a sex-offender record for the rest of his or her life. I tell my students that if a six-teen-year-old boy has intercourse with a fourteen-year-old girl, theoretically both can be convicted on statutory-rape charges.

I place even greater emphasis on the selfishness and immorality of it. "You have to sneak around," I say. "You lie to each other and your parents, hide and feel guilty about what you're doing, and go against every religious teaching that exists on this subject. Then you have to face the horrible decisions and life-long repercussions that come from both abortions and bearing unwanted children." I also emphasize the statistical finding that teen relationships that include intercourse fall apart more frequently than those that don't. I tell them that if they truly think they have that special someone they want to spend the rest of their lives with, they should have the self-discipline not to ruin the relationship by overcommitting physically and emotionally. Last, I warn them of the physical harm from sexually transmitted diseases that can come from being sexually active (I prefer the term "morally inactive").

I spend hardly any time at all on birth-control education, though I do tell students about common methods and I mention Planned Parenthood and free clinics. When they ask what they can do for 100-percent protection against sexually transmitted diseases and pregnancy, I explain that there's no foolproof protection because there's no right way to do the wrong thing. When all is said and done, the most effective method of birth control is a good education, living and teaching strong character values, and jobs, especially for girls.

I tell parents and teachers that self-disclosure is both effective and necessary if they hope to get through to kids in this area. They need to share with them their experiences of relationships that may have been ruined by premature sexual involvement and the resulting lying and angst. If they can do so truthfully, they might also contrast their own committed, loving marriages to such a ruined relationship and let the students see the difference.

When all such advice falls on deaf ears and children disregard what parents and teachers counsel (often because the kids smell hypocrisy in "Do as I say, not as I do" talks), no one should be surprised when problems arise. A parent's or a teacher's personal example underpins everything in the teaching or parenting of a child. It's not that children aren't learning anything about values. The problem is that for the most part they're all too effectively soaking up lessons from adults—learning perfectly from very imperfect examples.

Concerning drugs and alcohol, what I advise other teachers and parents is relatively brief and blunt: If you're using illegal drugs, you should be arrested and your children and/or your teaching credential should be taken away from you. If you're using our most abused drug, alcohol, to deal with your life issues and then scold the children because they, too, need help coping with life but don't happen to use the same drug as you, well, you're wasting your breath. What you're doing contradicts the scolding. Sure, you're an adult and they are children, but to them the age difference is irrelevant. All they see is the hypocrisy. By getting your own act together and keeping to a drug-free lifestyle, you'll be amazed at how successful you'll become at helping your students and your own children do the same thing. "You can't teach what you don't know" is as true of substance abuse as it is about teaching social studies or algebra.

Schools and Parents

- Practice the "Do as I do" rule. Anything less is dishonest and hypocritical. If parents and teachers—in fact, if all adults a child comes in contact with—were to behave as they would like children to behave, there would be no crisis in our schools and homes.

Rule #5

WE RESPECT PEOPLE
AND PROPERTY

At West Valley you get hands-on people skills. They
teach you to respect and care about other people. That
helps me now in working with kids that are autistic, [or]
have Down syndrome and other problems.

—Alice, 17, certified nurse's aide;
West Valley graduate; former dropout

It all starts with a kind of Golden Rule: I'll treat you and what
belongs to you the way I would like to be treated. We respect
people and property. Showing one another respect, if not love
and charity, is just good common sense to keep people peaceful, harmonious, and constructive. Such behavior is the chief
virtue of being civilized. The catch is that some people don't get
the message early in their lives. As children they're not taught to
respect others, nor to tolerate people who don't look, live, or
speak as they do. They either grow up in a bubble of ignorance
or are indoctrinated to hate anyone they see as a threat. And not

practicing universal respect is an explosive, destructive short-coming for anyone living in a country with a mixed population.

We teach West Valley students that there are three ways to respond to a stranger walking down the street toward you: ignore him, glare at him, or smile and say hello. My students admit that they almost always choose the first two options. Like much of their behavior, this response is most likely learned from their parents. We change this behavior in students by getting to the root of the problem and attacking its component parts.

Racial animosity is one primary cause. We hear stereotypes far too often: whites are racist and stuck-up; blacks are too loud and pushy or they are dope dealers; Latinos are illegals, gang members, or people talking trash about everyone else in Spanish; and Asians are totally cold and indifferent. To counter such flip and thoughtless generalizations, we work to get our students to avoid judging or acting toward others on the basis of outward appearances. This is a challenge because from what I've observed over more than a quarter century, by the time they enter school, most children already have their minds racially poisoned by their parents.

A sad example of this occurred while I was an assistant principal at Valley Center Middle School in northern San Diego County. This high-desert community consisted of luxurious small ranches, owned almost exclusively by wealthy white families, surrounded by four Indian reservations, where poor Indian and Latino children lived. One day I suspended a white boy for calling a Mexican child a "beaner." While waiting for the father to pick up his son, I was counseling the boy about how inappropriate and hateful that kind of language was. I thought

I was making progress when suddenly his dad barged into my office. A huge man at about 6'4" and 300 pounds, he was a local contractor, had a shaggy head the size of a buffalo's, and forearms the size of my thighs. He looked thoroughly angry. "Good," I thought. "He's really going to give his son a strong talking-to."

But instead of turning his head toward his son, he glared at me, his face red, neck veins bulging. "Why is my son being suspended for calling these Mexicans beaners?" he shouted. "That's what they are!" I'm not often at a loss for words, but I couldn't say a thing. I just motioned to the boy that he should go with his dad. As the man stomped out of the school office, I couldn't rid myself of the depressing thought that this boy (and countless others like him) had no chance to grow up with a sense of universal tolerance and brotherhood. Of course, white parents don't have a monopoly on teaching their children to be racially biased. I've repeatedly observed similar behavior on the part of parents of all races.

I tell my students and their parents that hating or fighting someone is what you do when you've run out of choices. The poor, the poorly parented, the unloved, the low-achieving students are invariably the ones who hate and lose their tempers the most. This is because in their minds they have so little and fear losing it so much that any change around them (including an unknown person entering their space) is perceived as a threat.

LEARNING TO RESPECT

Most of the teenagers who come to West Valley never got the message about respecting people and property. If they did, it didn't take. For all kinds of reasons, from poverty and ignorance to neglect and abuse, they come to me filled with festering anger against someone or something. Whatever they may have learned of respect was lost long ago in a fog of drugs, alcohol, and years of unbridled misbehavior, often abetted by gang life and parental misbehavior.

Despite the anger little Peter, from my Cooper Elementary years, felt from having so much difficulty in school, in time his anger dropped and he became an eager, agreeable kid who learned to respect my rules and even his classmates. Every child changes for different reasons. In Peter's case I believe mental toughness made his turnaround possible. He was strong enough to disregard what others thought or said about him and focus on doing his own work. Ultimately, he skipped two grades and caught up with his peers.

Kevin, the angry teenager I began helping in Detroit during my student-teaching year, was also mentally tough. However, he had to face another kind of prejudice. Short, slight, and white in a predominantly black neighborhood and school, Kevin was sometimes perceived to be gay because of his intellectual interests and his artistic bent. He seethed at those who picked on him and at any authority figure, including me. As his eighth-grade teacher, I had to eject him during his first days with me because he was rude and disrespectful. "You can come back," I told him, "but we've got to talk and figure this out first."

Kevin did come back and we talked. I discovered that his home life was a mess: an absent, drunken father and a barely functioning mother, driving Kevin to booze and narcotics. When on the spur of the moment I decided to help stop his self-destructive descent, I had no idea the counseling and mentoring would become the foundation for a lifelong friendship. Kevin's turnaround was gradual and involved his moving west and living with my wife and me almost as our son. Drug free and sober, he shed his anger and thrived because we showed him that we respected and cared about him.

When young people are making big changes in their lives, not all the issues that need resolving come to the surface at the same time. Nola's father and his home drug habit surfaced midway through her time at West Valley, threatening to derail her progress in leaving behind a life of drugs, gangs, and sexual escapades. I spoke to him and he promised to keep his pot habit away from his daughter. As for Frankie's problem, which had simmered for months under my radar, it surfaced as an allegiance to gang life. The Internet photograph of him posturing as a street-tough *cholo* brought the issue out in the open and I had to drop him.

Likewise, Carlos couldn't let go of the gang life and returned to it, which led to his doing time in a youth prison. In the cases of Frankie and Carlos, the positive work I did with them while they were with me was not lost.

Some students come to West Valley already having learned to

respect others, but the respect often is not returned. Racism is a form of one-way respect, and in my experience African Americans are the main victims. Chris came to me as an unusually well-behaved young black man. I couldn't begin to guess what had brought him to West Valley. Like roughly 90 percent of my students, Chris had grown up without his father. However, he was blessed to have a strong mother whose strength was not in the loudness of her tirades when he disobeyed her but in her commitment to enforcing strong values and principles.

Chris loved football, and coaches told him in tenth grade that he had a promising future as a college linebacker. But after the football season he lost his motivation for school, stopped attending classes, and allegedly started drinking and using drugs. In eleventh grade he was failing and ineligible to play football. Eventually, he dropped out of his local high school altogether to come to West Valley. He came to our school with no hope of ever rejoining his high school team and was resigned to graduating behind his class, if he graduated at all.

His first few weeks at West Valley went well, as we got to know each other and he grew used to our program. The first post-honeymoon meltdown occurred when he showed up one Monday morning with his head shaved. One of our primary school rules is that the boys don't wear their hair any shorter than a number two clip on an electric shaver. It's plenty short enough for them to have the hairstyles that are fashionable, but it helps keep their appearance distinct from the current gang look of total baldness. It also provides a normal appearance for their required part-time jobs. Chris knew I would immediately question him about the behavior violation.

After a few minutes of discussion with him at the lunchroom tables, where we congregate before going to class in the morning, it was obvious that he had not joined a gang. He was just so tired of trying to change his life drastically by attending West Valley that he had chosen baldness as a frustrated protest against all the rules he had to follow. That same afternoon, I met with Chris and talked with his mother. The conversation was brief and directed solely at Chris. My little speech went something like this: "Your mother works hard to provide a home for the two of you and she has to follow certain rules to keep her job. Here at West Valley, we have the autonomy we need to be able to provide wonderful help to kids who want to change their lives. But even with all our autonomy, we still have rules we have to follow if we want to keep our doors open. The same is true for students. You have countless opportunities here to get back everything you've lost. It's very possible for you to catch up on your grades, go back to your regular school, play football your senior year, and graduate on time."

Chris listened intently, especially when I added, "But you've got to follow a few rules. It's kind of like the legal term 'quid pro quo,' 'something for something.' You have to be willing to sacrifice a few minor things, like wearing your hair one-eighth of an inch longer than you might like to. If you make your sacrifices and commitments, then we will make ours. We'll do everything possible to help you achieve your dreams. I'm going to treat you like a man, and I don't want to ruin our relationship by nagging you about this. Tonight, think about what I said. Decide what you're going to do. I want you all the way into our system, being our absolute top student and leader. Or, I want you all the way out, which means I'll help you find a school with lower expectations and standards. Tomorrow morning, let me know what you decide."

With that said, the rest was up to Chris. His mother thanked me, and the next morning he came in and said he was "in" with the program. From that day forward, he behaved with the poise and integrity of a grown man. He achieved a 3.5 grade point average during his time at West Valley, becoming the only two-time winner ever of our Smartest Student Quiz Bowl Award. He caught up on his credits and went back the following September to play for his high school's football team his senior year. On the first kickoff of the first game of the year, his mother and I, along with his former West Valley classmates, were in the bleachers cheering him on.

A few weeks later I called Chris to see how he had played in another game, with a nearby private high school; it was a Christian Protestant school where most of the students and players were white. He sounded subdued and I asked him what was wrong. He said that after the game he and his teammates, who were mostly Latino and black, were going through the line shaking hands with the other team's players. "One of their players, a white kid, called me a nigger for no reason," Chris said. He implied that some of the other players and coaches had heard the remark and done nothing.

Living near the private school where Chris had played the game and always reading about the high ideals they espouse, I reassured him that he did the right thing by not responding. I said I would call the school and was sure we'd get an apology. But in spite of repeated calls, their football coach never responded. After far too many calls to the school principal, I finally reached him. All he had to say was, "Well, there's a lot of things said on the football field and we'll look into it."

Later, when I told Chris what the man had said, I praised the way his mother had raised him: to respect all races and never insult anyone in that manner. I also told him that just because a person has a college degree and a respected social position doesn't mean that he possesses integrity and good character.

Shortly after the football season ended, Chris called me at school one afternoon. He told me he was worried about being in the "looser" environment of his regular high school, which was dilapidated and affected by gang and illegal-drug influence. He said he wanted to return and finish at West Valley; he did so and graduated three months ahead of his senior class at the other public high school.

Black Americans unarguably continue to be the most disliked among all races, and I see distressing proof of this in essays written on a topic I no longer assign. For years, in a variety of school districts, I would ask students to write a brief opinion paragraph that answered the question "How racially diverse would you date and why?" Without exception, my black students almost unanimously wrote that they would date anyone they truly loved or respected. Color didn't matter. However, almost without exception, my white, Latino, and Asian students wrote that they had no problem dating someone from another racial or ethnic group but would never date a black person. When I asked these students why, the most common answer was, "My parents don't like blacks." I work to reverse this attitude among my students, but, sadly, in homes and schools across America, parent-driven prejudice continues. It must be stopped if America is ever to heal its racial wounds and redress gross inequalities.

REDIRECTING BEHAVIOR

My task is to get my students to understand and accept the basic rule about learning and practicing respect for people and property. I tell new kids that our building has clean, graffiti-free walls and our floors are unspotted by gum because no one defaces, litters, or defiles the school or anything in it. All students agree to respect the facility. If they don't they can't stay. But following the rule doesn't come naturally. It takes constant reminding on my part as well as exposure to the unfamiliar. Sooner or later the message penetrates: respect is when you appreciate or esteem someone or something; therefore, no defiling of property and no trashing people, no rudeness, no profanity, no sarcasm, and no personal or racial attacks.

This works well in the safe and closely watched confines of the school. But what happens when these kids leave for the streets, for home, for work? It's as if I've given them training wheels, hoping they can someday remove them and pedal on their own without falling. It really depends on how well I've "redirected" their previously destructive behavior.

The key to controlling and redirecting inappropriate behavior is timing, knowing when to intervene forcefully and when to make just a few gentle corrections. Envision a piano rolling down an incline. You're the only thing in its way to the bottom and you want it to go in a different direction. To keep from being flattened, somehow you have to meet the piano's momentum with an equal or greater force. To succeed, in the instant you stop the piano you must also shove it away, redirecting its path. When it's headed in the direction you want it to go, you can practically keep it going with just a few fingers.

It's tricky and dangerous, but the key to making inappropriate behavior stop is knowing when to intervene. The same goes for problem kids. I keep inappropriate behavior from escalating by catching it at the beginning. That's why with kids I'm always watching the small stuff. When I spot the tiny infraction, I douse the small fire before it grows into an all-out blaze.

One of my West Valley students got the piano-stop treatment at an amusement park. He was part of a group I'd taken on a holiday field trip to an amusement park. The grounds were packed with people and he was upset because some of the kids had taken off for a particular ride without him. He began yelling into the earpiece mike of a cell phone as he tried to guide the group back to the eating area, back to him, me, and two adult friends of the school who were with us.

"Softer, please," I said gently. "You're too loud."

He continued yelling, either not hearing me or ignoring me. Again I asked him, a little more directly, to drop the volume. But he kept shouting, "No! Not there, we're over here!"

I reminded him again and still he wouldn't stop. Initially, I think he was unaware he was yelling in our faces and drawing annoyed glares of those in the crowd around us. But when he kept on, I was sure he was simply acting out his annoyance with the other kids by bothering us and everybody else. I had reminded him to lower his voice four times, to no effect. I had hesitated to make a scene, but after the fourth request, I came up to him and shouted almost at the top of my voice, "Take that earpiece out! Speak more softly! You're screaming in our faces and it's rude!" I was tempted to shake him by the shoulders but my barking at him like a Marine drill sergeant was rebuke enough. Embarrassed and seemingly with all eyes on him, he complied immediately. The next day in class he quietly absorbed my lecture on cell phone etiquette in public.

On another occasion I successfully shoved the piano off its downhill course when I caught a high school boy trying to start a brush fire at my Potrero Hill Middle School in San Francisco. It happened on a Saturday afternoon when I was driving my pickup truck by the school and spotted three black teenage boys in the dry weeds next to the school building. It was a three-story, prison-like concrete structure with few windows, bordering a poor neighborhood. I saw the smoke they were fanning into flames, stopped the truck in the middle of the street, hopped out, and ran across the lot to the three boys.

I put my hand on the shoulder of the first boy I came to and said, "You're under citizen's arrest for arson." He pushed me away and I had to wrestle him to the ground, while he screamed that I was racist, that he was going to kill me, and that he knew where I lived. The other two boys were about to pile on and help their friend, but just then a man came walking by and I asked him to call the police. That's when the two friends ran away, and I managed to hold on to the third while stamping on weeds that were starting to burn.

"Aren't you being too rough with him?" a female voice said. "I don't think you have to hold him that hard."

I looked up and saw a middle-aged white woman nearby on the sidewalk. I was so caught up in my tussle with the boy and annoyed at the armchair quarterbacking that I blurted out, "Give me your address, lady, and the next time he wants to set something on fire, I'll send him to your house."

She walked on just before the police arrived. I explained what had happened and said that I was the principal of the school. Then one of the two officers asked me, "You don't really want to file charges, do you? You know how the courts are. He'll be released before we even finish his paperwork."

"You bet I want to file charges," I said, "unless you go get his mother and bring her to me in fifteen minutes so I can talk to the two of them." The cops agreed to my condition and left with the young arsonist in the back seat of their squad car. In ten minutes the police brought the boy and his mother back. I unlocked the school and we sat down in my office and talked. I asked the boy, "Why were you trying to do that to my school?"

He said he was mad because the previous year he was fired from his summer janitor job at our school by the head custodian. We talked a bit longer, and then, under his mother's watchful eye, the boy apologized and promised he'd never do it again. I discovered that he was angry a lot and was a poor student. I offered to get him some tutoring by calling his school and talking to his counselor. Before mother and son left I asked him one last question: "Why did you call me a racist? What did my color have to do with what you were doing?"

"Nothing," he admitted meekly.

"That's right," I said, "and when you're doing the right thing, you're welcome here at my school anytime."

During the following week, he started getting the tutoring he needed. I also decided to give him another chance, asking our custodian to hire him back for part-time work. In the end he worked for our school without a problem, and at his high school he became a better student. That would not have happened if I had not been willing to get involved, bolt across the weeds, and, in a sense, deflect the onrushing piano.

TEACHING TOLERANCE

Over the years, I've found that pouncing on the smaller lapses in propriety pays off when I attack attitudes of intolerance, where the degree of disrespect is even greater and more stubbornly resists change. This is especially true with teenage attitudes toward ethnic and racial differences.

As with respect, students *can* learn to be tolerant. At West Valley, I tell them not to give in to blind hatred toward people they don't know just because they belong to a population group they've always feared, demonized, or ridiculed. Bigotry gets passed on from one generation to the next, but it can be erased by a heavy dose of knowledge and exposure to different types of people. We shouldn't picture all Muslims as terrorists any more than we should see all Mexicans as illegal border-crossers or barrio gangsters.

One afternoon my students and I witnessed a scene made to order for stereotyping. We were returning to the school on a city bus after visiting a skid row shelter downtown to serve lunch to the homeless. Two black teenagers, about the same age as my students, had just entered the bus and drawn everybody's attention. With their pants hanging precariously off their butts, they were dancing and behaving in as foul-mouthed and rude a manner as anything Eddie Murphy ever lampooned on *Saturday Night Live*. Because of the way they were raised and the lessons their parents and teachers obviously had *not* taught them, these boys had steered their behavior to a point where they would be viewed as unemployable—even as a stage act.

Their shaky, hip-hop, falsetto voices rose above all conversation. They were in a bubble, maybe on drugs, but seemingly oblivious to all the other packed-in passengers, who were a mix of races and ages—workers, elderly men and women, mothers with little kids. Most everyone looked fearful or bothered. They would shake their heads or, like my teenagers, stare with open-mouthed expressions that seemed to say, "What planet are you from?" My students kept glancing at me to see if I'd tell the intrusive dancing duo to rein in their act. I thought about it, but our ride with them was short and I kept expecting normal inhibitions to kick in. That never happened.

Lewd and offensive, they were an embarrassing stereotype, the kind that's often spoofed by black entertainers and sports personalities. Everyone seems to give a wide birth to kids with this thuglike rapper look, or the skinhead neo-Nazi look, or the Latino bald gangster look. Best to say nothing rather than be called racist, people assume.

But what's wrong with America's adults speaking openly and frankly about teenage appearance and behavior in public places, where it's no longer a question of their right to individual expression and their choices become forced on everyone around them? For my part, I think there should be an enforceable, well-publicized standard for teenagers in public, one that respects general sensibilities and at the same time allows for individual expression. For those who think this sounds too extreme, consider that many theaters and shopping malls have been so taken over by this kind of appearance and behavior on the part of some teens that many potential shoppers and moviegoers stay clear of these places.

Over more than twenty-five years, all kinds of kids have accepted my behavior rules and standards, and I suggest they be used as a national model.

A NATIONAL MODEL OF BEHAVIOR STANDARDS

If children of all economic and racial stripes don't get a clear idea of acceptable behavior standards from home, school, or their religion, then I suggest they try mine. Implemented in every possible circumstance with teenagers, these behavior standards have never failed to bring positive results. Here are the topic areas and my comments, as I give them in class:

- Loud, in-your-face talking and blasting music are irritants, so we keep the volume reasonable.
- Profanity and vulgarity are incendiary, offensive, and impress no one; avoid them.
- Losing your temper is not brave and courageous but is a sign of weakness and fear; build your strength by increasing your willingness to talk about things that upset you.
- Drugs and alcohol reduce your ability to control your

thoughts and actions and encourage avoidance rather than brave confrontation with our problems; they'll weaken you.

- Avoid euphemisms for lying and stealing; it will cure you of both of them.

- Sexual intercourse is not a sport, and when you engage in it outside of marriage, you risk hurting others, yourself, and children you are not ready to provide for.

- Gangs are not an activity for anyone who wants to be a real man, because real men handle their own business, and gang members never do.

- There's no real satisfaction in having money that wasn't honestly earned; a job gives you a unique sense of worth as nothing else can.

- School's real value is that it teaches you skills you can use to help others; when you drop out, you're hurting the ones who are counting on you.

- Talking back to parents and teachers weakens you; build your strength by being respectful.

- Skin color is not an identity; go out and accomplish something and learn who you are as an individual.

- Don't be afraid to try different cultural experiences, to expand your world.

- There are no excuses for ever physically abusing or intimidating a woman or child; doing so is a symptom of a real sickness within.

- Never fear hard, dirty work; a grown-up with no work ethic is of little value.

- Always involve yourself in incidents you observe that

could hurt someone else; living with indifference and moral cowardice hurts you far worse and does more damage to you than any beating anyone could ever give you.

- You can't give yourself happiness, because it's the side effect of living unselfishly; to be happy, look for people in need and help them.
- If all your friends are the same color, sex, and age as you, you're full of prejudices and missing out on wonderful opportunities; examine the situation and find out why you're limiting yourself.

GANGS BREED RACISM

The influence of gangs and racial or ethnic "clustering" of kids in school cannot be underestimated. Gangs breed racism. Whether they're Latino, black, Asian, or white, each gang is racially exclusive. Gangs thrive on a mindless hatred of other gangs and this spills over into the classroom, cafeteria, hallway, and playground. For years I've fought the destructive, criminal gang lifestyle by offering kids more than an alternative to the dead-end promise of hanging exclusively with Latino homies, black gangsters in the 'hood, or white-power gang members in the suburbs.

Compared to the enticements of gang life, my way is not fast or glamorous. All it requires is a pure motive with no personal agenda. It starts with any kid who wants out of a gang or wants to get away from the pressures of joining one—and recent studies show that most gang members *do* want out. When such a kid arrives at West Valley, my first target is usually his intolerance and anger toward kids of other racial or ethnic groups. At the slightest sign of this kind of attitude, I'm on it in seconds. If I notice my Latino students gathering in a cluster or separating themselves from the several black students in the class, I bring it out in the open and we discuss what's going on. The last thing I want is some nasty, whispered remark or racist vibe infecting the classroom.

Our racial discussion rules are simple: One person at a time speaks. You can speak with emotion and bring up absolutely any concern you have, but you must keep your volume down. No cursing, racial slurs, or pejorative language are allowed, because that kind of talk inflames rather than enlightens. If a hard-core racist gang member (they're almost always one and the same) tries to make a power play and refuses to abide by these discussion guidelines, I remove him from the room firmly and quickly.

Once I have my students' trust that I'm impartial and that everyone will have a chance to be heard free of hateful comments, students not only become willing to talk about their racial feelings but also usually don't want to stop. As with discussions of most tough subjects, gentle humor at the right moment goes a long way toward easing tense moments and can be helpful in getting shy, hesitant, or angry students to participate in discussions.

Sometimes racist or exclusionary words and actions are so subtle that they can be seen only fleetingly in a glance or a frown; other times it's as bald-faced and open as a student calling another a name, labeling a mentally slow student with an epithet, or mocking someone's religion.

For example, one group of kids might be kicking back in our rec area listening to rap on the school's boom box before classes start. Another group of first-generation Latinos may be speaking Spanish and keeping separate from their more assimilated brethren who don't speak Spanish. Suddenly, someone replaces the rap CD with a disc of Mexican *ranchera* music. When I hear the groans and whining, I tell them, "Get over it! The world offers us all kinds of music, maybe not beautiful to you but to someone." I never let them complain. If I did, they'd start clustering off on the basis of tastes, hairstyles, shoes, skin color, or anything else that separates them.

SPEAKING TO THE GOOD IN PEOPLE

Not long after I arrived to be vice principal at the Valley Center Middle School in San Diego County, vandalism and drug-fueled fights between two gangs flared up. The fights seemed to be rooted in racist emotions between Indian kids from the nearby reservations and the kids of Mexican descent. The conflict had been going on since their parents' days at the same school.

Hoping to stop the violence, I brought two leaders of both gangs into my office one day after narrowly preventing a knife fight between the two groups. I had no idea what I was going to do or say, but I figured it couldn't hurt to get the leaders talking to each other. The boys, all about fifteen, were facing expulsion and were probably expecting a hard-core blast from me. I knew their families a bit and knew that they occasionally went to

Catholic or Protestant churches. So I took a stab and said, "You've gone to church before, right?" They nodded.

"There's a prayer you've all said," I continued, "It starts with the word 'our.' What's the next word?"

After a moment, one of them said, " 'Father.' "

"Good. Now, was he white, black, or brown? Whose father was the prayer referring to?

"Everyone's. He's everyone's father."

"All right," I said, "if that's so, then what are all of you guys to each other? What's your relationship?"

The boys looked at each other with puzzled expressions. Then one of them said, incredulously, "Brothers?"

"Exactly." I let it sink in, and then asked, "You've got brothers, right?"

They nodded, still looking puzzled.

"You've all fought with your brothers, true?"

More nods.

"When it starts getting out of hand, how does your mother get you to stop fighting? What does she say?"

One kid frowned and answered, "She says, 'He's your brother, for Pete's sake! And this has got to stop!' "

"Well," I told them, "that's all I've got to say to you today. These boys, too, are all your brothers, and the fighting's got to stop."

I ended the meeting there, and the boys hesitantly shook hands and went back to class, still amazed that I wasn't holding them for possible arrest or expulsion. There were no further outbreaks of this type of violence during the remainder of my time at Valley Center. I eventually left for another job, and almost a decade later I heard from a staff member that the school still remained free of major incidents.

The best solutions are always uncomplicated and direct, and that was how this situation turned out. The boys went back to class having admitted to each other that there was no justification for continuing their hatred of each other. They didn't have to try and save face by continuing the feud. For my part, I had set the school's standard to a level of no tolerance for any gang activity, so that subsequent administrators had to hold fast to what was working. This is how good rules and real principles work, I tell educators and parents. It takes a great effort to get them in place, but once you do, if you consistently and impartially enforce them and avoid exceptions, these rules will deliver a campus that promotes learning and transforms kids' lives.

What worked was something I learned to do when I first got the hang of dealing with troublemakers. I just spoke to the good in that group of boys. The two gangs had been stuck on some kind of racism or tribalism for generations. That animosity appeared to perpetuate itself blindly and without good reason. Hatred had become a tradition. I simply spoke to their sense of brotherhood, as viewed in their families' religion.

LESSONS IN RESPECT

I've always been quite open in class about how I was first schooled on respect and racial intolerance, mainly because my students can relate to the story. The year was 1968, and I was sixteen and living with my parents in the mostly white Detroit suburb of Farmington. I loved playing basketball, but the only good pickup games I could find to hone my moves were in the nearby city of Pontiac. One night as usual I borrowed my dad's '67 Nash Rambler and drove over to the black housing projects until I found the right action at a school gym in Pontiac. The neighborhood looked trashed and absolutely poor and was considered very dangerous for me, the only white guy around for miles.

For some time I had found good games in Pontiac and simply shrugged off any safety concerns. That night, eager to play, I left the car in the school parking lot and hurried inside the gym in my game shorts, T-shirt, and white Converse high-tops. At six feet, I was strong and confident I could play with the locals.

I approached some kids waiting their turn and asked to get into the next game. They nodded and showed me some attitude. As soon as I told them my name, they laughed and started calling me Whitey. But I'd grown used to the nickname on other courts, as well as to their rough style of play. In fact, I welcomed it. Such bruising workouts were improving my game to the point that I would soon be named a Michigan all-state high school player.

I got into the next game and more than held my own. Afterward, I slapped hands with a few of the guys, said good-bye, and headed for the parking lot. I was alone, and as I walked across the asphalt I saw a half dozen boys hanging around the Rambler. I found out later that they belonged to the Devil's Disciples gang. They glared at me, but it wasn't anything I hadn't experienced before. I got into the car, but as I started to drive off, a chunk of concrete hit the trunk.

I stopped, looked in the rearview mirror, and saw one of the kids, the smallest, winding up to heave another chunk of concrete. This time it crashed onto the hood. Without thinking ahead, I opened the car door and raced over to the boy and grabbed him by the arm. I started to take him back inside the gym to complain to the supervisor. Just then, one of his bigger buddies yelled, "What are you grabbing him for?" At the same time, another gang member I hadn't seen knelt down behind me, so that when the first Disciple pushed me backward, I tumbled to the ground.

As soon as I hit the asphalt, they jumped on me. They pounded away, punching and kicking. I tried protecting myself by curling up and covering my face. There were too many of them for me to fight back, but somehow I stood up and staggered over to the school building, fending off blows as well as I could. My back was against the wall and the punches continued.

Just then a Good Samaritan in the guise of the man supervising in the gym came out of the building and said, "What's going on?" He got between me and the boys, but I could see more guys, some with baseball bats, coming up from across the parking lot. I figured they were going to finish the job. Then my rescuer, who was black like everyone else, told me, "Kid, I'd suggest you get in your car and get the hell out of here!"

Even though I was in pain and my face was bleeding, I bolted for the car, hopped in, and drove off slowly, trying to get my emotions under control. It was dark and I was passing some apartment buildings, when all of a sudden a black Lincoln Continental came speeding up behind me, swerved around my car, and cut me off against the curb. All four doors opened and four guys with baseball bats jumped out and came for me. I put the car in reverse and headed backward at top speed—in reverse that was about seven miles per hour. In retrospect the maneuver saved my life, because when I saw the guys running toward me, I knew I couldn't escape them going backward, so I put the Rambler in first gear and floored it. I went right at them. They jumped out of the way and then ran back to the Lincoln, got in, and chased me as far as the white part of the city.

With my face all puffed up and bloody, my body bruised, I drove home seething at the guys who'd beaten me for no good reason. I wanted to kill them. I was hating all black street punks. Even though I'd stopped at a friend's house to clean myself up before I went home, when I walked in the door of our house, I gave my parents a jolt. Then I told them the story. My mother helped me finish cleaning myself up, and the next day in the kitchen she said, "Well, thank goodness you're never going back there."

"What do you mean?" I shot back. "There's a game Friday. I've got to be back there!"

"No," she said softly but looking very concerned. "You can't do that."

I started yelling: "You're not going to tell me what to do! I'll go back there! I've got to go back there! You're ruining my future! I'm going to be a pro basketball player!"

Just then my father walked in. Never one for long lectures or many words, he simply looked at me and said, "Stop. You're never going to talk to your mother like that again in this house. If you do, you're going to leave."

"Good," I blurted out. "I'll leave."

"Fine," my father said in an even voice. "Don't let the door-knob hit you on the way out."

Still sore, I limped to my bedroom, stuffed some clothes into a gym bag, and left. At the bank, I withdrew what I had in my savings account—about two hundred dollars. Then I called friends. I told them what had happened and asked if I could stay with them for a while. In so many words, my white buddies all turned me down. Then I ran into Tyrone, a black kid I knew from high school ball. I told him the story, and without hesitation he invited me to stay with him.

I moved in with Tyrone and his grandparents in the all-black part of nearby Ferndale. In their small, threadbare house, I shared the attic with Tyrone. His grandma immediately treated me like another grandson, feeding me what she had, washing my clothes, and introducing me as Tyrone's "white brother" to friends and neighbors who stopped by. Tyrone's mother, I learned, lived in a house across the street with his brothers and a sister, a beautiful kid I ended up dating for a while.

Because Tyrone was one of the best ballplayers in Detroit—a big handsome guy, friendly with everyone, especially the girls, black *and* white—I started thinking I was just as cool. I tried to imitate a more hip walk, something we called the pimp walk. We'd move along singing Motown songs and trying to harmonize. I probably looked like Steve Martin in *The Jerk,* but I didn't care because Tyrone and his family had absorbed me into their rhythms, ways, and culture. Compared to my own restrained, toned-down family, Tyrone's world seemed so much more lively and spontaneous, warm, and generous. I loved it. At one point, I even wished I *were* black. It was during this time that I learned the essence of respect: People are people first. All else—like race or baldness or wallet size—is secondary.

I tell my students that I learned several things after I ran off to play basketball in Pontiac: I got a painful dose of racial intolerance when I was pounded by black punks. But that led to my leaving home and gaining a lifelong affinity for African Americans and other people of color. I lived with Tyrone and his family at an impressionable age, and the love they wrapped around me has far outlasted the beating I got that night at the playground.

I also learned more about respect in my own home when I returned to my folks' house after several weeks in Ferndale. I'd been grossly disrespectful to my parents, yelling at them and disobeying my father's number one rule: Obey the rules of the house or leave. I apologized for my behavior, they embraced me, and life went on. I never again disobeyed them in such a blatant way.

At West Valley, I've imposed the same standard as my dad had at home: Respect the house rules or leave. Some kids get it right off. Others, like Whitey, who itched to play ball across town, learn it the second time around.

Schools

- Enforce a Golden Rule: Respect other people as you want to be respected.
- Ban all racist talk on campus, including the usual name-calling and slurs.
- Prohibit all signs of gangs on or near campus.

Parents

- Teach respect and tolerance to your children by setting an example of such behavior at home.
- Redirect inappropriate behavior (intolerance, lack of the most basic respect) by correcting it immediately.
- Avoid using hateful, racist talk around your children.
- Keep gang members away from your home.

Rule #6

WE LIVE CLEAN AND SOBER

I can't remember when I've been this happy. Since I
came here I'm getting right with my family and friends,
I'm off the drugs and staying out of trouble. I'm doing
really well in school and I've got a job. That's the
coolest thing.

—Kathy, 15, West Valley student;
former crystal meth user

We live clean of drugs and alcohol. This rule, *No* drugs or
alcohol, is an easy one to remember, but it's a tough one
for parents because it's meant for them, too. Most parents drink
alcohol socially, if not regularly at home, and many routinely
smoke marijuana and self-medicate with various kinds of pre-
scription and illegal narcotics. In my experience the single
biggest determiner of whether or not a child uses drugs or alcohol is the parents' behavior. That's why I ask for parents to
help me with this rule at home. It's not enough to get the par-

ents to warn against drinking and doing drugs; they must quit, too. For most of my students that means Mother is on the line, since in many cases Father is absent and out of the home picture.

If I were a teenager and heard my mother criticizing my drug use while she's sucking on a beer or wine cooler, I'd probably ignore anything she said. Attempts to argue that her drug is legal and socially acceptable while mine is not come off as complete hypocrisy. The message would be that I have to deal with life's challenges without chemical assistance, whereas she is unable to do it without her drug of choice.

Parents who think this restriction on their own behavior is too extreme need to be aware that one mistake on their children's part with drugs and/or alcohol can kill them. So anything less than the best parent role modeling they're capable of exponentially increases these lethal odds. For such parents, finding a position on this issue is a bit like trying to answer a financial planner who asks, "How much risk are you willing to accept?"—only in this case the risk may cost the life of a son or daughter. To the degree that parents tolerate their children's use of drugs or alcohol, and use them as well, to that same degree they increase the likelihood that they or their children will be done in by disease, mental breakdown, spousal abuse, incarceration, or premature death.

With illegal drugs, the argument to ban all use is easy. They're all illegal, addictive, and dangerous to some degree, and their use and trade attracts a criminal element. As for alcohol, you might ask what harm a small amount would do. The truth is that alcohol is far more pernicious than drugs: Drinking kills many more people annually than all narcotics combined. I hear the argument that young people should be allowed to drink "in moderation." I disagree. Anything that destroys so many lives is evil and I don't believe evil can be taken in moderate doses, especially by teenagers in this age of binge drinking and no restraints.

Some otherwise responsible parents believe that if their children are going to drink, they might as well drink at home where they're safe. Such parents are incredibly naïve if they believe the drinking goes no further than the home. From what I've seen, this kind of soft approach to alcohol consumption *never* limits what kids do elsewhere with their friends. Letting a teenager imbibe at home is usually a weak parent's attempt to gain a kid's acceptance. It sends a message of wholehearted endorsement of drinking and is the best possible way to start a teenager on the road to alcoholism.

The same holds for parents who believe that a bit of "experimenting" with drugs is a normal, robust part of growing up. They may see smoking a joint or snorting coke as a product of youthful curiosity or as a coming-of-age ritual like the ones they themselves went through when they were teenagers. Whatever the reason, such permissiveness needlessly takes lives and ruins the future of countless children. I ask that all my students' parents, at least while the kids are young and impressionable, not behave as cowards. I ask that they take the unpopular stand and swim against the stream of declining social values. Because their children run the highest risk among teenagers of abusing alcohol and drugs, they must take the lead. Doing the right thing in this case is not even a matter of morality; it's a practical matter of keeping their children sober, safe, and intact.

At West Valley, I can't really monitor parental drug and alcohol use. What I can do is appeal to the parents' sense of right and wrong and their love for their child. For example, one boy, eighteen, came to me with a history of years of drug abuse. Ernie was on probation for possession of a deadly weapon; as well he was on the verge of serious gang involvement. He stopped the drugs to stay at West Valley, but one Monday during my usual "rounds," when I checked on students' weekends, I found out that he was now drinking alcohol. With his father's willingness to supply beer at home, he'd switched from drugs to booze abuse.

I called the father immediately and insisted on his presence at school that same afternoon. Arriving at my classroom door, I called the son and father together and stepped out into the hallway for a five-minute conference. "You love your son," I said, "but what you're doing by supplying alcohol is going to cost him his freedom and possibly his life. Ernie's underage. He's on probation. Drinking is illegal for him. If you really love him, and I know you do, you will stop giving him alcohol."

Ernie's dad teared up, looked at his son, spoke with him for a moment in Spanish, then turned to me and said, "I won't buy any more beer. I'm sorry." The dad has kept his word, and the results speak for themselves. Ernie, who was a high school dropout and a borderline gang member when he arrived, now has a driver's license and his first job, has gotten off probation, is clean and sober, and has pulled back from the gang life. He also is enrolled in a vocational class, has become a motivated student, and is about to graduate from West Valley.

CRYSTAL METH CLAIMS SIX GIRLS

Every Monday morning when I do my "rounds" in the class, asking each student what he or she did over the weekend, I usually can gauge whether they have stayed alcohol free. Mostly, I rely on their honesty and their general appearance and behavior in class. When a kid is alert and calm one day and overly hyper and irritable the next, I know something's wrong. If I suspect any drug use, I ask whether they want me to run a test to screen for the major drug families. A random, voluntary practice, it involves a five-dollar urinalysis dip test that I pay for myself. It's not paid for from school district funds and it's voluntary. By law I can't force anyone to take it, but 100 percent of my students and their parents agree to testing.

When I have a student I believe is using, it soon becomes obvious. Sometimes a student will admit he smoked pot or took a hit of crystal meth or coke at a party, in which case we'll talk it over. Suspension, getting dropped, a heart-to-heart, a follow-up screen in a week, a visit by the parent or parents—any of these are possible outcomes. Continuing with some sort of sanction depends on whether I believe the kid can benefit by staying at West Valley. They know I don't want to find out through a test that they've been using. I want them to tell me if they slip up. That's why I've written a permanent message on the chalkboard that shouts to them, "No Surprises!"

To hear their side about the drug tests I do on them only underscores the need for voluntary testing. Here are two typical statements by former drug- and alcohol-abusing students. Written by girls, they are responses to my questions about why they came to West Valley and what keeps them in the program.

I was failing high school because of my bad attendance. Out of eighty days in a semester, I missed seventy-one. I would disrespect my mom. It got to the point where I would even push her around. What was causing me to mess up is I was doing crystal meth with my friends and I didn't really care about school.

The part of the West Valley program that has helped me is the drug testing. When my first drug test came out dirty, I felt embarrassed. I had lied about it, saying I wasn't using. So I decided to stop. Now I have a job in retail sales, a night class in keyboarding, I respect my mom, and my drug tests come out clean.

Before coming here, I was ditching school, starting in ninth grade. I was going to kickbacks and drinking so much that I was risking my life. Because of that, I was failing everything.

Since attending West Valley I've been doing really well. I have a job in a restaurant, a savings account, and I took an auto mechanics class last semester to catch up on my credits so I could graduate from West Valley or go back to regular high school and graduate with my friends. I'm doing much better in school by coming every day and paying attention.

The part of West Valley that made me change was the

drug-test and the fact that I can talk to Mr. White about my problems at any time.

I didn't always have a random-drug testing policy. But in 2002, just when I was toughening the rules for staying in the program, six girls changed my mind. They were all friends and lived in the same neighborhood within blocks of each other. They were sweet, pretty, and polite. When they started coming to West Valley together, they impressed me with their smarts and capabilities. Whatever the lesson—math, current events, U.S. history—they were with me. After several months I noticed all six were falling off in their class work. My questions about drugs only brought earnest, cheerful denials. Finally, their performance in class, deteriorating behavior, poorly explained absences, and my suspicions uncovered the truth. They were addicted to crystal methamphetamine and habitually lied about it.

Disappointed, I bounced them from school and then reassessed my policy about drugs. Instead of merely suggesting they not use drugs, I began a zero-tolerance policy with random tests.

In the years since the six crystal meth girls left, I've kept up with their lives enough to know that the drug seemed to rob them, sucking out the promise of a good life from their tweaked-out minds. I watched them stagger through a series of continuation schools, sitting and staring blankly, knowing nothing, underemployed or without jobs, and running with thugs who cared little about them and ultimately got some of them pregnant. If only one of the girls had come to me and said, "I'm feeling weak. Help me," I could have done something. But while they were at West Valley, whenever I asked them how they were, they slid away with lies and vague smiles. Soon I lost my hold. If they had been honest, I could have helped them. They might be drug-free today, enrolled in college classes, working at good jobs.

Sometimes as I'm driving through their neighborhood, one of them—a cigarette or a forty-ounce malt liquor in hand—will wave and shout, "Hey, Mr. White!" from a junked-up yard through the weeds and broken chairs.

I slow down and ask, "How's it going?"

"Same-o, same-o . . . you know."

"Take care, dear," I yell and wave good-bye.

The memory of what could have been hurts. These girls lied their lives away for a habit they wouldn't break, one that destroyed their brains—because that's what crystal meth does. I can do nothing more for them, so I drive on. I can only focus on doing all I can to help my present students, whose lives still hang in the balance.

The sad story of these six girls makes the case for early, strong, no-nonsense intervention with drug issues. The many girls I've lost, almost exclusively to crystal meth, really wanted to get out of that life. They knew it was killing them, but they weren't strong enough to make a stand on their own. I gave them all the support I could on the school end, but if the home situation is weak, nonexistent, or drug infested, the school's efforts are outweighed and addiction claims another victim.

Nola, the student whose father had drug issues at home, told me that she quit drinking and smoking pot when she came to

West Valley. She eagerly volunteered to be tested and was proud of what she called her "new me." Six months before her graduation, she heard about an entry-level nursing program at the local vocational center that sounded promising. She applied, was accepted, and completed the program's three grueling months of study and on-the-job training. She took a break from our school to work the full-time vocational program at local hospitals, study for her anatomy, first-aid, and other tests, all the while working thirty to forty hours a week at a restaurant. Much of what she earned went to support her mother and sick father.

During this time, she came to school to see me one afternoon. "I just can't do it, Mr. White," she told me in tears. "My dad's smoking marijuana. It's in the house and everywhere. I know I'll test positive just by breathing the air at home."

She was afraid she'd test dirty at West Valley and have to be dropped and not graduate. She was upset and worried. But more than that, she was deeply disappointed that her father and mother were not backing her up in her effort to change her life, to leave the pot, alcohol, and partying gang life. The support wasn't there.

That's when I called and got her father's promise to drop the dope at home. He kept his word and Nola finished the program and got her nursing assistant's certificate.

As with gangs, where drugs are concerned I won't negotiate. Drugs are like handcuffs or ankle chains, but the restraints are chemical. Addiction is a chemical restraint. Before I can help you, you have to admit you have a problem. If you don't, we're both wasting our time. As it is, we waste too much time, money, and human energy trying to help people recover from addiction, people who don't really want to break the habit or won't admit they are addicted. There's little or no point in wasting time on kids like the girls on crystal meth who no longer wanted to change.

WHAT SCHOOLS CAN DO

If leaders in public education truly want to tackle the problem of alcohol and drug abuse in schools, they must tackle it head on. They must immediately enforce a zero-tolerance rule for the presence of alcohol, narcotics, and all other illegal non-prescribed drugs. They can do this by carrying out the following policies at all middle and high school campuses:

- Any students exhibiting bizarre emotional or physical behavior should be suspected of being under the influence, should be sent to the principal's office, and should have their lockers and possessions searched (all entirely within the law).
- Their parents should immediately be called in and the school should offer or insist on a drug screen or breathalyzer test on the spot (these tests cost little and can be done in under five minutes).
- Students testing positive should immediately be suspended and have a police report filed on them by the school.
- These students should be required to attend some sort

of counseling and should be warned that repeat behavior will result in expulsion.

In the rare instance that a parent does not want to test a child thought to be under the influence, the school has the legal and moral right to file a child abuse report on the spot (it's more than a coincidence that parents who balk at testing are typically those who are drug users themselves). The critical point is that teenagers are not "little kids" but rather are on the verge of adulthood. So behavior that is overtly bizarre and possibly drug related at their "place of work" (the school) is highly inappropriate and must not be tolerated, for their sake and the sake of the community.

A strong, consistent stand of this sort will immediately restore order, respect, and a positive learning environment to any campus. By drying up the pool of users, it will also automatically cleanse campuses and the adjacent streets of drug dealers. I believe dealers are the true evil in the world of substance abuse among children because they prey on kids' mental weaknesses, often destroying them just to make money.

I had one boy at West Valley when we first opened who finished his last few credits with us, and eventually graduated with our full support. I remember he was having a hard time getting his post–high school life started and asked to come visit his former classmates at lunchtime. Shortly thereafter, I learned he had tried to sell cocaine to some of them right on the property.

I liked him and had invested a lot of time and effort in getting him his first job. But wrong is wrong is wrong. Dismissing his lame apology, I wasted no time. I called the store owner I'd originally talked into hiring him, told her about his attempted drug dealing, and recommended that she fire him. Then I called the police and filed a criminal report. The police went to his house, questioned him, and since he was on probation they searched him and his home. Charges were filed, but the case never went to court. It was, however, the last time I saw him near our school. I think he gave our school a wide berth after the police warned him that a conviction would have meant more than a decade in state prison.

Although I feel badly about this young man's moral breakdown in trying to sell dope, and I regret our lost friendship, I accomplished my top priority. I'm keeping the campus free of drug dealers and sending out on the street the clear message that, without exception, we stand up for our school rules and seek prosecution to the full extent of the law.

In a cabinet at school I keep an envelope of pictures of students I've dropped. I think of the collection of color glossies—photos we shoot of all students on their first day at West Valley—as "the morgue." Now and then I go through all the photographs; I remember each student by name and in my mind can see their faces long before I open the envelope. I still feel close to them, especially the boys who did actually die of gunshot wounds, drug overdoses, or crimes gone bad. The twin evils, drugs and gangs, are the reasons most of the photos landed in the morgue. I meditate on this every time I attend an ex-student's funeral. I want to cry out and lay blame but don't, out of respect for the grieving relatives and friends. Instead, I focus on live students, on what I can do to steer them away from a similar fate.

LEAVING THE FOG OF WEED

Ernie, the kid whose father promised to stop giving his son beer, is a big boy, his size belied by his gentle personality and soft-spoken speech. When he greets people, he smiles and gives each one a hug. He sits in the first row, to my left, furrow-browed as he tries to jot down everything I say. He's new at West Valley, and needs the better part of a year to graduate. After three years of smoking marijuana six to eight times a day, he obsessively writes everything in his lined notebook because he's worried he won't get his memory back as sharp as he'd like. Weed does that to the brain, which is why he came to me as a special education student.

He sits in the same row of students where Nola and Marla used to sit. Both girls were familiar with him before they came to West Valley, and in their way their stories helped big Ernie stay clean. Forming something of a support group, most of my current students sympathize and frequently talk things over with him. When it comes to most problems in a new student's past, there's just about nothing the kids haven't heard or done themselves. A kind of in-the-battle-together feeling permeates discussions about drug and alcohol abuse.

Ernie had been caught for drug use and possessing a weapon, and a judge sentenced him to a year's probation. He'd never been arrested and in jail before, and this scared him enough so that he quit marijuana and focused on doing well in my class. He told me he originally drifted into fringe involvement with the gang life because it was easy to do and no one was pushing him to study or give him any direction. Now, he's a dishwasher at a local restaurant, where he works with his dad, a busboy at the same place.

When Ernie first came to my class he spoke haltingly, was fearfully shy, and seemed to want to disappear into his big body. Because my rules encourage students to treat newcomers as they would close family members, Ernie soon had no trouble fitting in. His speech became smoother and he started smiling and laughing. His most frequent comment became "I love this school."

As he writes, his face down close to his notebook, I end our usual morning review of newspaper headlines and top stories. Then I say I'd like to announce the winner of the month's Most Improved Student award. I first describe the winner as a "friendly young man with a big heart and a bigger mission in life. He came hoping to change his life and he's already taken huge strides toward that goal."

Then I mention Ernie's name. After a moment, he stops writing, raises his head, and suddenly realizes he is the winner. I ask him to stand and hand him the official-looking framed certificate. As the former pot addict takes it and thanks me, I see he's beginning to grin and cry at the same time. We all applaud and later he tells me the award is the first thing he's ever won in his life.

"You didn't win it," I say. "You earned it."

LEARNING IN A SAFE AND PEACEFUL PLACE

Since most of my students have struggled with past drug and alcohol problems, offering them the choice of a new life at West Valley means providing them a safe, clean, and peaceful place to be and to learn. This kind of environment is a fundamental requirement for us if we're going to work at getting to the causes of their past misbehavior. Some newcomers immediately take to classroom learning, something most had abandoned years ago. These students are as eager and committed as Rhonda, the tiny dynamo who led the school choir and even wrote her own solos, or Nola and Marla, who both arrived at West Valley hungry to learn and improve themselves.

On the other hand, some students attend class day after day but remain disconnected. They're so attached to the attitudes, habits, and posturing of their street persona that it takes some time for them to connect to classroom learning. It can and often does happen in an instant. Suddenly, they're engaged and feel the rewards of knowledge. I remember one boy, a classmate of Carlos, at Mid-Valley Community Day School, my so-called "monster" alternative school. He was such a student.

When he came to the school, at seventeen, his life was in free fall. A member of the Long Beach Crips, the same gang Snoop Dogg publicly promotes, he'd been incarcerated repeatedly for drug-related crimes, had a miserable upbringing, and now wore the classic stony-faced scowl of a sullen hard-core gangster.

One morning in class I was emceeing a word game; as in *Jeopardy*, the kids could holler out answers. The Crip, a smart boy, reluctantly started participating in the game, calling out a few right answers. He saw he could do it and before long he ended up in the championship round against another kid. All my usually lethargic students were suddenly amazed at seeing this side of the boy. They were sitting up in their seats cheering for him. He, too, was leaning forward, hands excitedly gripping the sides of his chair.

I asked the final question, he shouted the right answer, and all of a sudden he had won. The room erupted in sincere cheers, and in that instant an incredible change came over him. The thuglike demeanor dropped, the faux-adult act disappeared, the anger and stress melted away, and his face broke into this wonderful, beatific smile. For a moment he seemed luminous. It was like lifting the flap of a tent to peek inside before it drops back down. I glimpsed a boy who knew there was something else to life, something that felt good. Ever so briefly he savored a satisfaction and integrity he'd never known before.

His flash of normalcy was the first of many such experiences in the months I knew him. The scowl and strut left him, he began to enjoy learning, and drugs and booze faded in his life as habitual problems. I lost track of him after he returned to a regular high school in Long Beach, but I can only hope he's found a permanent kind of integrity in a non-gang existence.

When students like the Crip have that turning-point moment, their bodies appear to relax and their whole affect changes. They seem to physically morph into kids who carry themselves differently, walk differently, and speak differently. Suddenly, they're normal young adults, not teenagers pretending to be hardened thirty-year-olds. I see this every day at West

Valley. And when I ask them what's going on, what *are* they feeling, they'll say something like, "I feel peaceful. I feel safe here."

Schools

- Enforce a zero-tolerance rule for the presence of alcohol, narcotics, and all other illegal nonprescription drugs on campus.

Parents

- The example of drug and alcohol use in the home sooner or later endangers the young and impressionable witnesses of this behavior. To protect your kids, the biggest sacrifice has to be made by you. Stop your use, at least until they're young adults, and you will have taken the greatest possible step toward helping your children stay clean and sober.

Rule #7

WE LIVE WITH COURAGE

> [Mr. White] pushes you in everything. He sits down and
> works with you, puts you on a higher level. All you have
> to do is show him you'll do what it takes, and he'll
> definitely be on your side.
>
> —Anthony, 22, salesclerk; former West Valley student;
> former drug user and convict

We live with courage so that we can make a difference in
our own lives and the lives of others. But courage demands sacrifice. I work with my students on understanding the
principle of sacrifice involved in many kinds of courage, from
the grit and pain needed to finish a set of push-ups, sit-ups, and
squats to the moral pluck it takes to confront a bully twice their
size. In both situations they sacrifice comfort, although taking
on a bully also requires a strong moral conviction that a wrong-
doer must be stopped.

I explain to my students that most of the time we operate

with a kind of courage that gets us through our day, one task at a time. If we persevere and have a goal in mind, most likely we'll accomplish what we set out to do. Practiced daily, this determination to move ahead will become a habit and even a confidence that anything is possible. I sometimes meet intelligent young people who seem to have been born with a surplus of such can-do courage and spirit. Yet when put to the ultimate test, they fail. As a teacher, I try to puzzle out why certain people have the heart and stamina to overcome life's bigger obstacles, and others don't.

I helped convict Carlos with my statement to the authorities about his continued gang activities. However, during the time he spent in a youth prison I always believed that despite the abuse and poverty in his childhood, despite his family's history of gang ties, despite all the bad habits, arrests, and setbacks, Carlos fiercely wanted to change his life for the better. I knew he wasn't the "Godfather" tough guy he pretended to be in the back row of my "monster" school, Mid-Valley, trying to intimidate the world. Underneath the stony expression was an intellectually curious, congenial, and determined young man.

We exchanged letters during the first year he was locked up, but then he stopped writing. One day, after I hadn't heard from him in more than three years, he called. "Mr. White, it's Carlos," he began brightly. "I'm out, off parole, and guess what? I'm married to a wonderful girl and I'm working."

"Congratulations," I said and I think he could hear my smile. "I'm really happy for you."

"I'm also taking a few college classes and want to take some more."

Listening to him talk excitedly about all the progress he was making in turning his life around, I could hear his pride. I didn't even think to ask him about the courses he was taking, what he was interested in pursuing as a career, and where he was working. I was just listening to the joy in his voice.

"It must have been tough getting things right," I said.

"You always said it takes courage. I just called to say thanks for that."

"Don't thank me. It's all you."

Not too long after that call, I invited Carlos and his new bride to dinner at our home with my wife and me. As is our custom, we joined hands to pray as we sat down to eat. I was about to say something, but no words came out. I looked up at Carlos through a growing mist of tears and finally said, "Carlos, I thank God for letting me live to see a day that I never thought would come, a day when you and I would sit down together as free, responsible men and share our blessings together."

Carlos then added sincerely, "I never told you this but you were like a dad to me. I appreciate it."

Like Carlos, another young man I helped also had done prison time. I met Ricardo more than twenty years ago, in 1985, while driving in Northern California early one Sunday morning. He was hitchhiking and I pulled over to give him a ride. He hopped in my pickup and we started talking. About eighteen, Ricardo recently had been released from a juvenile prison, where he had spent four years on a felony assault conviction. I asked him if he planned to work and he said he wasn't sure. "I'd like to go to college but I don't know," he added, explaining that while in the California Youth Authority prison he had earned a high school completion certificate. I was impressed because the proficiency exam to get the GED certificate is not that easy. "Did you study a lot?" I asked.

"No, I just took it," he said.

Instinctively, I felt Ricardo could probably turn his life around quickly if he were given some direction.

"I'll tell you what," I said. "I'm going to the state college to sign up for some classes tomorrow and I think I have a way to get you enrolled, too. Would you like that?"

His face lit up.

"Be at my house at six tomorrow morning," I said and gave him the address and directions. I told him 6 A.M., thinking that if he was truly interested in improving himself, he'd be on time even at that early hour.

The next morning he showed up at six on my front porch, ready for the long drive to the college. Handsome, clean-shaven, and nicely dressed, Ricardo looked excited and eager to seize the day.

At the college, I had some free time to help him get started, so we began at the registrar's window. "Can I see your transcript?" the woman behind the counter asked him. Ricardo, in a polite but matter-of-fact voice, said he didn't have a transcript because he'd been in prison for four years for having run with a gang as a gangster thug. "Would you say you're historically disadvantaged?" the woman asked. "Has your family had a hard time?"

"You bet," Ricardo answered, "every social problem there is."

The clerk then sent him to another line, for the Education

Opportunity Program, and after a counselor there finished with him, Ricardo had a full four-year ride assured at Sonoma State University—if he stood in one more line. That was the line to take the Scholastic Aptitude Test Saturday morning, two days away. It was a formality, the counselor said; his score wouldn't even matter. But Ricardo had to take it in order to receive a needy-student scholarship, which would cover tuition and books.

A building contractor friend of mine offered to give him work whenever he wanted. It didn't matter that he was a convicted felon. As for lodging, I arranged for him to stay for free at a women's shelter in exchange for some custodial and gardening work. In just a very short time out of prison it was as if this smart and bold young man had hit the jackpot. His life was about to turn around. All he had to do was show up to take the S.A.T. Saturday morning.

But he didn't. Ricardo blew off the whole thing by getting drunk the night before and missing his testing appointment. Though he looked to me like a smart and confident winner, I believe that in the end he didn't have the courage to go through such a big change in his life. He knew college was the right path to take, but perhaps he was afraid to leave old habits and learn new ones. Despite possessing greater natural talents and opportunities than Carlos, Ricardo failed where it really counted. He lacked the heart and desire to truly change his life.

The last time I saw him, several years later, Ricardo had spiraled down. Originally from the California central valley city of Stockton, he had come out of a poor, gang-ridden neighborhood and now had returned to the street life. I remember when I first knew him he used to brag about walking around town carrying a shotgun underneath a full-length "duster" coat to shoot up the other gangs. Still into gang life, he probably was still carrying the shotgun.

He told me he had crashed his car into a telephone pole while driving drunk and showed me where he'd knocked out all his teeth. No longer bent on self-improvement, he borrowed ninety dollars from me, supposedly to fix his teeth, and disappeared. I never saw him or the $90 again.

SACRIFICE BRINGS ITS OWN REWARDS

Most West Valley parents deeply appreciate what I've done for their children. Sometimes they tell me this in tears. But their own bad habits—such as booze and sometimes drugs—are so deeply ingrained that they forget *they* have also signed on with me to turn their kids' lives around. Certainly, I'd like parents to quit whatever they do to self-medicate. I ask them to make this sacrifice to help their kids. But often the best I can get from them is a promise not to encourage their sons and daughters to fall back on their old destructive ways.

Unfortunately, in our present culture of quick gratification, sacrifice is seldom seen as a virtue, as something you do in order to succeed. It's practically become a bad word. We've stolen the lessons of sacrifice from children by teaching them that you sacrifice only when you make a mistake. Yet throughout history people and whole societies have succeeded and advanced by sacrificing their time, money, labor, luxuries, even their lives.

Sadly, parents who will not sacrifice for their children by spending more time with them, by caring for them, pass on to their offspring their own attitude of selfishness.

Schools reinforce this state of affairs by not teaching kids enough about the benefits of personal sacrifice. Rather than emphasizing material wealth and extolling celebrities or inventors who've struck it rich, why not focus on the selfless acts and lives of people like Mahatma Gandhi, Albert Schweitzer, or any number of local heroes? By keeping sacrifice away from children, not just as a concept but as a reality in their own lives, we encourage them to become self-indulgent adults obsessed with physical appearance, uncaring about others unless there's personal gain.

I tell my students that when they lose their willingness to sacrifice, they lose everything. They become cowards. For example, giving up an afternoon to weed their grandmother's garden requires physical effort. Standing up to a muscle-bound bully when they see an injustice done also requires effort as well as moral courage. I ask them to push the limits to do the right thing, to take a stand, to exceed expectations, even if it's just to do ten more sit-ups during our exercise drills. Summoning the courage to sacrifice comfort during calisthenics takes only a tiny amount of effort. Giving up an ingrained, destructive habit such as drug and alcohol abuse is a much greater sacrifice because it requires a ton of moral strength and courage.

My parents, especially my mother, first taught me the benefits of courage and sacrifice, starting when I was about five. She insisted on piano lessons for me and I didn't want to cooperate. We would argue all the time over my having to practice every day for at least a half hour, and longer as I grew older. One day my dad couldn't stand the ongoing tug-of-war and blurted out, "Forget the lessons, Elizabeth! You're ruining your relationship with Paul. And you're driving me crazy. Why make him do it?" Cool as could be, my mom answered, "Because once he's into it ten minutes, he stops arguing and enjoys it. The day he stops enjoying it, I'll stop."

It was true. After a while I stopped whining and I did enjoy playing. At West Valley I pass this and other Mom-inspired lessons on to my students. For instance, when a kid complains about not wanting to do something good or right and parents give in, it's as if they believe the saying "You can lead a horse to water but you can't make it drink." My favorite teacher would say, "Hold him there long enough and he'll drink." The same goes for kids. You don't let them off the hook just because what they're doing is difficult or boring. Today I enjoy playing the piano because years ago my mother realized she needed to be the adult and not have her child try to run the show.

She pushed me on just about everything except playing basketball. In a way, my father took care of that. I was about fifteen, and one afternoon he was watching me shoot baskets in our driveway. I'd been throwing the ball at the hoop for a couple of hours. "Why are you practicing so much?" he asked me.

I stopped shooting and answered him very earnestly, "I've got to earn a scholarship to play college ball."

He shook his head and looked at me in disbelief. "Son," he said, "you're just not that good."

His words, which were a simple statement of fact and were never meant to hurt, actually drove me to practice even more. His remark motivated me to outpractice everyone on my high school team, to the point where I not only played on the first-string varsity squad, I starred, and made the all-state team in my senior year. To my father's amazement, I even won a basketball scholarship to Florida State.

Compared to most players, I wasn't as fast or as tall and I couldn't jump as high. But success is not always determined by natural abilities. You've got to want to attain your goals enough to sacrifice anything and everything to achieve them. I suppose because I had such a commitment to my athletic goal, I didn't mind endless hours of practice every day.

Motivation, I learned from that experience, is everything. When kids are afraid of the unfamiliar, when they have to go for their first job interview, or when they're facing a big test to qualify for some kind of training program—say, nursing or electronics—I often share my basketball story. "Do you have the desire and courage?" I ask. "If it's something you really want, take the test ten times, or a hundred times, if you have to. You'll study and you'll pass it. It's just a matter of when."

Rhonda, the little dynamo who was West Valley's first female graduate, never lacked motivation and courage. Though she's no longer at the school, I tell my current students about her habit of seizing the moment. Her spirit is behind a sign in class that announces in bold letters,

IDEAS WON'T KEEP.

SOMETHING MUST BE DONE ABOUT THEM.

"When you get a notion to do something good, do it," I say, "or the moment's gone and you're thinking of something else." I remind them about this constantly. I have to—because with children, unselfish notions definitely don't keep. There are critical windows for acting on ideas and they can't be delayed until a more convenient time. Impulses to do kind or generous deeds must be acted on immediately.

Rhonda would plunge into activities almost without hesitation. With the same zeal and dedication that she ran the choir, she built her own successful curb-painting business. She'd walk through neighborhoods with her stencils and cans of spray paint, knocking on doors, and because she was so persuasive she could earn several hundred dollars a day from painting address numbers on curbs.

But what I most admired about Rhonda's lack of hesitation was how quick and constant was her care of Suzy, one of her seven siblings. An incredible amount of Rhonda's time went toward caring for Suzy, a younger sister who was profoundly mentally disabled; most families would have institutionalized her. But Rhonda never saw Suzy as a burden, loved her deeply, and included her in her activities as much as she could. Suzy in turn worshiped her older sister and as a result didn't misbehave as she might have without such love and attention.

In the same way that love motivated Rhonda to care for her disabled sister, incredibly high levels of desire and self-discipline drive certain artists and athletes. In class we read about the courage and sacrifice shown by champions like the cyclist Lance Armstrong or any number of people who've reached the top of their field through desire and hard work. Sometimes I use an example that almost none of them are familiar with. I describe the greatness of the violinist Fritz Kreisler. I tell them

Kreisler, born in Austria, as a curious small child had a facility for playing the violin. In fact, from the age of seven he made learning to play the violin his primary goal and dedicated his life to playing the instrument. He emigrated to America as an adult and rose to be one of the most praised violinists in the world.

Then I tell my students the story about a woman who rushed up to Kreisler after a concert. Breathless and enthralled to be in his presence, she cried out, "Oh, Mr. Kreisler! I'd give my life to play as beautifully as you do." Kreisler instantly replied, "I did."

MY HEROES SHOW THE WAY

Two of my students showed me two faces of courage, one born of fearless innocence and the other rooted in a desire for freedom. The hero of my first story is Alex, my pint-size worst student ever, the troublemaker in Angel's class at Cave Elementary, the one I drove home to his mom in 1981 for a talking-to that got his attention.

One Friday night, as a treat, I took the entire sixth-grade class to a Chuck E. Cheese pizza restaurant for some snacks. A group of husky-looking high school kids, probably football players, was standing off to the side. One of the boys casually walked over to the counter display of candies, plucked out a handful of licorice, and sauntered back to his buddies. Alex, even though he was one of my littlest kids, walked up to the big thief and said for all to hear, "I saw you steal the licorice. Put it back."

At first the big guy denied it. Then, after Alex looked up at the boy's glowering face and repeated himself, the kid threw the licorice on the floor and ran out the door. I'd been watching from a distance and when Alex returned, I clapped him on the back and said, "Way to go, Alex! I saw that. But what made you do it?"

He looked at me as if I'd lost my mind and said, "What are you talking about, Mr. White? You always teach us that if something wrong's going on and you see it, you've got to do something about it." Decades later, I still wonder at Alex's example of moral courage. He didn't even consider that he was giving up a hundred pounds when he took the high moral ground and faced up to the thief.

My other story is about Sam, a slender, friendly kid whose family had come from Cambodia. A member of an Asian American gang, he was heavily into drugs and alcohol before he came to me. But in a matter of weeks, he dropped the drugs and drink, began to like his studies, and seemed to bask in the school's safety. After a year with me, Sam finished the West Valley program at seventeen. At the graduation ceremony I gave him a hug, but I had reservations about his future. I sensed that he still had an anchor in his life that was holding him back.

A week later he dropped by the school and proudly informed me that he had "officially" left his gang. "Wow," I said. "I'm proud of you." I didn't need to say more because we both knew that you almost never hear of a guy leaving a gang unless he's dead.

He said he had called a meeting of the thirty-five members and they had gathered in a big garage or warehouse where they wouldn't be bothered. Standing at a table in front of the group of boys and young men, Sam took off his bandanna, removed his cap, and put them on the table. "It was a ritual," he said. "I told them, 'Guys, I'm getting out.' " Then he turned around, heart pounding, and started to walk out. He was fully expecting they would give him the beating of his life. If he was lucky, he'd live without a crippling, permanent injury.

He took a few steps, and the leader shouted, "Aren't you forgetting something?" Sam turned, this time expecting a bullet through the chest or a baseball bat over his head. To his amazement, one by one the gang members came up to him and embraced him, wishing him well and saying things like "Awesome" and "Hang in there."

Sam stood up to the gang hype and pressure and was willing to take the consequences. He walked away with his integrity and body intact. That took enormous courage. When I repeat the story in class, I also tell the kids that if a gang still claims them and they want to cut the ties, they should call me. I've written my cell phone number on the chalkboard and they know they can get me at any hour of the day or night. "We'll take the beating together," I say, "and when the dust settles, you'll be a free man." They know I'm telling them the truth. I'll be by their side. But: "Courage," I remind them, "just gets you in the game. You've got to follow through."

DOING SOMETHING DIFFERENT

For people like Lance Armstrong or my former student Sam, courage demands total commitment. Quitting a drug habit also requires that kind of single-minded desire and purpose. My students with past drug problems can't afford to slip. "Drugs mess with your head and ultimately your whole behavior," I explain. "If you're using and coming to school, we're wasting our time. It's counter to everything we're doing here. You test dirty, you're out. You either quit or we quit you."

It's as plain and direct as the message on the wall of our main classroom:

If you always do what you've always done, you'll always get what you've always gotten.

They know they were screw-ups before they came to West Valley. Deep down they also know they don't want to return to that way of life. Until they get their bearings, they're in a kind of limbo between their old ways and the new way, which they've only begun. My job and that of any teacher trying to save lost kids is to make the new way so attractive and enriching, they're not even tempted to look back. If I've changed their hearts, if I've really helped them make genuine growth, then they can't return to what they were any more than an oak tree can turn back into an acorn.

For my students, most of whom have never traveled beyond the nearest hill bordering their L.A. suburb, summoning courage can be a daily challenge. Often, among some kids, life beyond the hills, beyond what they know, can be a frightening prospect. Yet overcoming such fears is also part of the courage muscle they must exercise at West Valley.

"We're going on a camping trip up the coast," I told the class one afternoon. Nola and some of the other girls perked up at the news. But other students, boys and girls, frowned with concern. During my teaching years I'd seen such expressions of budding fear on the faces of so many kids whose busted-up, poor families never took them to the beach, the mountains, the zoo, or an amusement park. They had grown up and lived their entire lives in the same place.

"All right, guys, think about it," I continued. "A gorgeous, cool, and shaded forest, a perfect beach, a river with fish and all kinds of birds flying around. In the day it's warm and sunny. At night it's quiet and you can see millions of stars. You get away from hearing gunshots at night, sirens, helicopters, and your next-door neighbor through the wall beating up his wife. You get away from the hoods hanging out by the cars. You get away from all that, and what happens?"

"It's quiet," someone answered.

"Yes," I said, "but there's more. You get perspective. You see more of the world."

Another boy said, "But outside of school, a lot of us don't know each other."

"You will before the trip is over," I said. "Whenever you go camping, you get to know each other real well. You cook with each other, you eat with each other, you brush your teeth with each other, you wash up with each other. Sometimes you get to know each other a little better than you want, but you need that experience. You need to know that in the things that really matter, we're all pretty much the same. It's a lesson that will help you in getting along with people in your future jobs and in everything else."

By the time we left on the rented bus to go camping, my students had shed their worried looks and were eager to try this new experience. They took forever to figure out how to assemble pup tents, and then they carefully visited each person's new "apartment," as they called them. These hardened city kids also ran up and down the beach, laughing like small children until they were exhausted. Later, at night, they played flashlight tag, scared each other with stories of unseen mountain lions, toasted marshmallows, and sang around the campfire. Two days later, unburdened of their fears, no one wanted to go home.

Schools and Parents

- Reward or recognize moral courage in children every chance you get.
- Celebrate the personal sacrifice that's often involved in helping other people.

WE CARE

What's helped me the most at West Valley is the drug testing, the counseling we get about what's right and what's wrong, and the fact that we have to do our best to help ourselves and other people.

—George, 18, West Valley student;
former pot smoker and habitual truant

We care about others. Compassion and unselfishness are muscles. They're like biceps, I tell the class. If you don't exercise them, they atrophy. That's one of the reasons I require all my students to have jobs. When parents have raised a child who has never engaged in activities that help others, they shouldn't wonder why the child turns out selfish. They should be no more surprised than if their kid never took a math course and couldn't do algebra, or ate a lot, never exercised, and was obese. Kids learn and do what they're taught. Compassion is an acquired capacity that becomes a habit; it's not something you're born with.

If you want kids to grow up to be compassionate adults, you have to teach them to think outside of their own needs and desires. An uncompassionate person is like a farmer who harvests all his corn for his own consumption and doesn't store any away for sowing. After he's finished eating his corn, he has nothing left to plant, becomes bankrupt, and goes hungry. He has no friends to feed him and his neighbors have turned their backs on him. To avoid the farmer's plight, kids have to be taught always to take part of what they receive in life and reinvest it in the lives of others in order to ensure their own continual supply of life's truly important creations. It's not just sound agricultural practice; it's also good living.

Marla, my once-foul-mouthed middle-class student with the wildly dancing mother, came to West Valley never having worked or done chores for anyone. Mostly she had drifted around the drug and gang scene, skipping school, overeating, and lacking direction. Her mother and her mother's boyfriend were doing the typical minimal supervision of her life, what I call "virtual" parenting, which is hardly any parenting at all. In such families, or virtual families, the children and adult figures don't have much to do with each other. The kids are like boarders. They make or get their own meals, retreat to their rooms, and come and go as they please. In such a home, it's no wonder Marla drifted off without purpose.

To satisfy my rule about doing part-time work after-school, Marla began doing volunteer clean-up chores and errands at a nursing home for seniors. From what she revealed about her life, it was obvious she had a big heart for the downtrodden, both human and animal. She loved dogs, had a scruffy, little mutt, and was always befriending strays. At the nursing home, her concern for others quite naturally blossomed. With a warm smile and a gentle toughness about her, she grew close to the seniors, even the crusty ones. When I asked her how things were going with the old folks, she talked about them as if they were longtime friends. She made no complaints as she spoke excitedly about their lives and some of the stories they told her.

Marla also lived near a much-used neighborhood park that gave her more opportunities to reach out to others. Recently landscaped, it now had two basketball courts where many of the local Chicanos would play or watch basketball games. Next to the courts was a grassy area the size of a football field where dozens of homeless—mostly illegal Mexican immigrants—would gather to drink, buy and sell drugs, gamble, argue, occasionally fight with each other, and keep a disinterested eye on the perpetual basketball games. They would also maintain a claim on a section of the grass where they intended to sleep that night. With a dumpster at one end, a portable toilet at the other end, and a water spigot in between, this park was a homeless addict's heaven.

Arriving at school one Monday, Marla told me she had walked through the park on her way to school that morning, enduring the inevitable whistles and rude comments from the homeless immigrants. She wasn't complaining, but was mentioning this daily scene only because she was concerned about someone else. "Mr. White," Marla said, "there's a homeless woman there who's living all alone." She looked at me expecting a suggestion of what to do.

"Why don't you ask her what her name is," I said, "and then invite her to come to school with you and talk to the class."

Marla looked surprised. "You think she would?"

"Doesn't hurt to ask. Tell her that your teacher will pay her twenty dollars to tell us her story."

The next morning, Marla arrived with "Nancy," the homeless woman, who was white and in her late forties. She wore a bright red pullover sweater covering multiple layers of clothing, and she was carrying two bulging black plastic bags. Ironically, Nancy was a former schoolteacher from Connecticut and had no problems with either drugs or alcohol. She simply had not been able to cope with a long and severe bout of depression, had lost her job, drifted away from her family, lost the car she originally slept in when she moved to California, and was now numbered among the most endangered of homeless species: the single, uncompanioned woman.

Nancy was somber but alert and sweet. She amazed the kids with her fearlessness when she spoke matter-of-factly about having to fend off would-be lovers, thieves, and rapists on almost a nightly basis as she lay sleeping under a tree in the park. After her talk in class, she stayed for lunch and continued having a good time with the children. We took a group picture with her; then, as when Cinderella's coach turned into a pumpkin, the school day ended, the students went home, and it was time to return Nancy to her park. Only Marla, Nancy, and I remained in the building.

A heavy, cold rain was beginning to fall, and I told Nancy that we would give her a ride "home." Driving over to the park in my pickup truck, I slowed down and instinctively asked Nancy where she would like me to drop her off. She didn't respond immediately, and in that embarrassing moment Marla and I realized that to the homeless, there is no "home" to get dropped off at. "Oh," Nancy said, "you can just drop me off anywhere; it doesn't matter." I pulled over to the curb, let her out the passenger side, and then handed her the two trash bags full of her belongings. Driving away in the downpour, Marla and I slowly waved to the unmoving, bedraggled figure. She didn't wince or rush away to find shelter but stood there, stoically enduring the downpour, as a horse endures an icy storm in an open field.

"Mr. White," Marla said, "we have to do something to help her."

The next morning we invited Nancy to go on a field trip with the class later in the week to help out at the Midnight Mission, on skid row in downtown Los Angeles. Nancy said she'd go, but only because she wanted to work with us doing volunteer help (serving meals, folding laundry, mopping floors). When we got to the mission, Marla and I gently suggested she talk to a counselor about getting into the mission's rehabilitation program for the homeless. Nancy consented, and within minutes was working out the details with a counselor, who assigned her a warm, safe bed and a slot in a job-training program. Nancy then joined us in serving meals. When it came time to leave, we hugged, said our good-byes, and filed out the front entrance. Marla was the last to leave; she was beaming.

A few days later, I was passing back history tests to my students. Marla saw that she had failed yet another one. She sighed and looked dejected. "Mr. White," she said, "I'm a failure. It seems I can't do anything right."

I told her that I knew the book work was hard for her and that it's definitely important to master it, and that I knew she would if she just kept at it. But as far as failure or success are judged, I told her, "Marla, in my mind, what you did for Nancy, literally saving her life from the streets, is more valuable than all the A's I could possibly give you. To me, you're not only a success. You're an inspiration."

COMPASSION AT BUTCH'S HOUSE

I first learned about compassion when I was six or seven. At the time I was just a witness and a not participant, never thinking it was anything but normal behavior. Only years later did I realize just how precious is an awareness of other people's suffering and the desire to relieve it.

When I was a boy, every summer my parents, sister, and I visited my father's family members in the town of Tipton, Missouri. We'd drive down from Detroit and always stopped at my uncle Maynard's house. He had a son, George Maynard, older than I was, whom everybody called Butch. He was born with cerebral palsy, so his body was twisted and spastic and he had no intelligible speech. He couldn't even sit up by himself. Most people would have institutionalized someone like him at birth, but not Uncle Maynard and Aunt Helen, Butch's main caretakers. Aunt Helen got him up in the morning, gave him a shower, shaved him, dressed him, and moved him around in his wheelchair. There wasn't anything she didn't do for him.

In the kitchen they tied him straight up in his wheelchair and rolled him to his place at the table three times a day so he could eat his meals with the family. Everyone talked to him, and Butch joined in the conversation with a kind of mumbling. He understood everything we said. You could see it when his eyes would light up. He just couldn't answer us in any way that I could understand, even though my aunt seemed to be able to figure out what he was saying.

Aunt Helen fed him because he couldn't hold silverware in his permanently twisted hands. She'd feed him with a spoon the way you feed a baby, wiping his mouth as she talked to him. After the meals, they'd lay Butch on a carpet in the living room and set down a bunch of toys and things around him to keep him amused. We'd come in the house and each of us would get down on the floor and greet Butch. He'd hold out his clenched fingers to shake hands with you, smile a lot, and mumble something. Everybody would come and go, stepping around him without a thought that he was anything out of the ordinary. My aunt and uncle were as proud of Butch as they were of their other child, a daughter.

For fifty-three years, until his death, Butch lived this way with his family at home. They saw his presence as normal and treated him accordingly. Whenever we visited, I just assumed this was how you treat a kid when he's yours and you love him. It's what you do for someone who's different and can't do things on his own. I'll never forget my aunt and uncle for all the tireless attention and love in action I saw them giving Butch. I now think that Aunt Helen was a saint first and a mother second, or maybe there's a saint in all good parents.

Sure, she loved her son, but it required much more than love to do what she did day after day for fifty-three years. She embodies the kind of person the writer Madeleine L'Engle must have had in mind when she wrote, "Love isn't how you feel; it's what you do." Of course, I don't expect all my students to adopt homeless folks as projects in compassion. But I remind them that empathy can often trigger compassionate responses.

MY FIRST LESSON

My first lesson in caring was instigated by my mother when I was about ten. I was so self-absorbed that even though I may have seen another person's pain or discomfort, like my cousin Butch's, I don't recall ever being moved enough to do anything about it. Mom changed that.

It was summer, hot and humid. School was out and I had every day just for myself. I'd been sitting around the house, bored and restless. All the time on my hands wasn't satisfying my hunger to do something, and the more I thought about it, the more dissatisfied I felt. My mother made suggestion after suggestion, all of which I flatly rejected. I was in a sour, dark mood and certainly didn't want Mom messing it up even more. Finally, she looked at me for a long moment and said, "Honey, the only thing wrong with you is, you've been thinking too much about yourself. Come on, let's go down the street. Poor old Mrs. Sherman is sick and stuck in her house with all this heat—"

"So?"

"Well, she needs her lawn mowed and can't do it by herself. You can do it."

"Aw, Mom!" I whined. "I don't want to mow her dumb old lawn!"

"Sure you do, son, and just watch, you'll feel a lot better."

I'd never heard of anything so crazy. How could mowing a lawn make you feel better? I didn't have much time to figure it out because the next thing I knew my mother had me by the hand and we were out the door walking down the block to Mrs. Sherman's place. Mom explained to her that I wanted to mow her lawn, which was just fine with her. My mother left and I went around the side of the house to the garage to get the mower. Hot, sweaty, and feeling sorry for myself, I pulled it out and rolled it up the driveway to the front yard. Reluctantly, I started pushing the thing back and forth over the lawn.

About ten minutes later, Mrs. Sherman came out with some cookies and Kool-Aid for me. The next thing I knew, my dark mood had vanished and I was feeling good, even happy. Mrs. Sherman couldn't have been more thankful. I could see my being there cutting the grass was making her feel better. The cookies and juice helped, but I actually felt good about helping her. I liked being congratulated for doing something unselfish, and the lawn-mowing experience that summer was the beginning of how my own sense of helping others developed.

Our schools don't teach caring and compassion regularly. Teachers have to expose the kids to situations where they have an obvious choice to help someone in need. It takes awhile to click, but it has to be done regularly. Again, it's like muscles not being exercised. If you suddenly work them out, the next day they're sore. How do you get rid of the soreness? You work out again and again. Soon nothing is sore and you can work out painlessly. The workout makes you feel good, even euphoric.

That hot summertime when I was stewing and waiting for happiness to come to me, it didn't happen until I did something, until I was pushed into an act of self-sacrifice. Happiness or a pleasurable feeling came to me only after I helped old Mrs. Sherman find hers. It happened again because my mother repeatedly made me do good things for others: mow lawns, carry groceries, paint fences, whatever little thing she spotted that needed doing. Eventually, the habit caught on. I liked the tips, but more important, I liked helping people in need, which in turn made me feel good about myself.

WAYS TO TEACH COMPASSION

There are many activities parents can use to teach their children compassion and care for others, and it's never too early to teach these lessons. Activities can include: preparing and serving meals to incapacitated neighbors; helping to serve meals at local homeless shelters; "adopting" a local family that lives in a shelter; participating in community improvement projects, such as street and park cleanup projects.

When parents show kindness to others in need, such an act is a priceless lesson for their children to see. One of my boys, from a poor but intact family, came in to class Monday morning and told me in glowing terms about something his mother did. They were all watching TV on a cold, rainy Friday night when they heard a knock on the front door at around 9 P.M. When his mother opened the door, there stood a crying, bedraggled woman they'd never seen before, with two small children. She was running from an abusive husband and they had no place to stay.

My student's mother immediately brought the strangers into the house. While she and his father tried to help the mother, he had the responsibility of caring for the two kids. He led them into his bedroom to watch TV but discovered that they were too young to get interested in the movie he had been watching. So he switched off his show and put on some cartoons that the younger children would like. Then he shared some chips and other snacks with them that he'd been planning to keep all to himself. Eventually, the two little ones snuggled up to him and fell asleep. My boy felt good about his time with the kids and said it wouldn't have happened if his mother hadn't invited the woman in. "I guess it's more fun to share," he added.

It's an absolute truth: You learn what you're taught. My mom, a teacher from the time she was sixteen until she retired at sixty, used to say, "The best thing you can teach children is that if they do something, there's always a consequence." When I personally busted a kid on the street for spray-painting a wall and with my cell phone made a citizen's arrest, the boys with him were shocked because they were not used to anybody getting involved. They were used to tagging without consequences.

I try to be the same way in class, focusing on consequences of bad deeds as well as good. If a jealous girl does something selfish, destructive, or hurtful, such as start a false rumor about another girl, she risks being dropped. Yet if she volunteers to help a new student get started on the computer, I thank her. Afterward, I see she's feeling good that the new kid is getting the hang of setting margins and trying out typefaces for doing the assignment.

CONNECTING COMES BEFORE CARING

As we did on our field trip with Nancy, several times a year we visit skid row shelters to do cleanup chores and serve hot food at the steam tables to a parade of derelicts, drunks, and addicts. Of all ages and every imaginable racial mix, they include disabled men and women in wheelchairs as well as mothers with children. We hear some of their stories, and the ones that seem to stick with my students are the tales of redemption and compassion. One man gave us a particularly poignant account of his round trip to hell. At age forty-two he escaped to drugs after his three-year-old daughter died in an accident. He couldn't face life without her. He became hooked on heroin and the drug eventually cost him his job, his wife, and his relationship with his other two kids. He became a homeless addict for almost ten years, finally surfacing in a courtroom where the judge gave him one final chance at rehabilitation.

"I hit bottom," he told us, "so there was nowhere to go but up. I've been clean now for almost two years." Aware that some of my students have had drug problems, the man explained that he now helped run an anti-addiction program at the shelter. "A lot of people helped pull me back," he added. "I'm just doing what they did for me."

Senior centers and nursing homes are other places where

compassion and caring can be openly practiced. I take my students so they can hear the stories of the residents, write letters for them if they can't manage it themselves, and read to them. Mainly, my kids comfort them just by their conversation and presence.

In return for our cheering-up visits, a group of patients at one nursing home agreed to judge a writing contest I held for my students. The title of the mini-essay they were to submit was "Someone Deserving." The winner would receive one hundred dollars from a local charity to give to the subject of the paper. All the submissions showed heart. Despite the occasional spelling, grammar, and punctuation errors, the message of the following passages from the three top entries reveal typical concerns of the entire class:

> *There is a family that I see a lot when I'm at the bus stop. It is a mother and son. The mother is always looking very dirty. The son has long blond hair that reaches the middle of his back; at first I thought he was a girl. then I found out his name was Scott and he's about ten years old.*
>
> *I never saw Scott's father until about a week ago. He came up on a bike and gave the mother a kiss. He was also homeless and had a lot of cans on both sides of his bike. I assume that he cashes the cans in and gives money to the mother to support Scott. I don't think they have a house, and I see Scott wear the same clothes a lot.*
>
> *Sometimes I see Scott and his mother walking because they don't have the money for the bus. They seem really in need of some money. I feel like crying when I see them, and*

I think they should get this money so they can get some decent clothes and a nice haircut.

—Johnny, 14

My aunt has to support herself and four kids because her husband left her. She has two jobs and yet doesn't have enough to keep her home the way she'd like to. It's sad because every Christmas she has to lie to my little cousins about when Santa Claus is going to come because she can't buy presents for all of them. I hate it when they see other kids on Christmas Day with new toys. My mom always gives them clothes but clothes don't make kids happy.

My aunt cries a lot sometimes from seeing her kids wanting things and not being able to get it. She feels that she does so much for nothing. The oldest kid comes to my house to collect cans. He will calculate how much he would get for each can and depending on that, he would give his brothers money.

—Maria, 15

I think my aunt Georgina deserves some help. I look up to her because she's a young (23) single mother and tries so hard to be both father and mother to her two kids. They are 7 and 3. . . . What I heard from her daughter and son is that the lady that takes care of them hits the young kid. He cries in the mornings because his mother takes him to this lady.

The daughter says the lady doesn't give her food. Sometimes I take the kid out to the park to play and just have fun.

*The kid loves me a lot and so does the girl. They have almost
no food in the fridge, so they come over to our place to eat.
[My aunt has] been hurt a lot because her husband left her
for a bartender/stripper lady. So now he says that the kids he
has with my aunt Georgina are not his so he doesn't give her
money at all.*

*The daughter is traumatized because she saw her dad
trying to stab her mother with a house knife. And now the
kids hate their dad. Sometimes I sit down and just cry because I see the kids with the same clothes just living a tough
life. . . . Knowing that the dad was addicted to cocaine and
drinking and tried to kill the mother in front of the kids is
scary.*

—Yvonne, 15

Again, as with tending wet concrete, the most critical period
in shaping children occurs early in life. The farther along they
go in the learning process, the more set they become in their
behavior and attitudes. In my experience I've found that the
older they are the more unlikely are the chances of changing
them at the core. And the changes they do make are increasingly on the surface and cosmetic in nature.

Sometimes I can work on a kid for months, thinking, for example, that I'm turning around a nasty street punk of sixteen
into a righteous, model student. Then one day I find out the ex-
gangbanger is still friendly with his fellow thugs and that all
along he's been playing me. It did happen.

Salvador, the son of a struggling single mom, came to West
Valley just after turning seventeen. In fairness to him, he lived

on a street where, with few exceptions, a teenage boy has only two choices: become predator or prey, victimizer or victim. He was smoking weed regularly, had never had a job, and had been expelled from his high school and put on probation for participating in racial gang fights, even though he claimed not to be a formal gang member.

Within a few months of attending West Valley, Salvador was drug free, was taking an auto mechanics class at the local vocational center, and had just been promoted to cook in a Mexican restaurant. He now had several thousand dollars put away in his first-ever savings account, from which he'd withdrawn enough to buy his mother some new furniture for their tiny apartment. To say the least, I had become fond of this model, motivated student.

As usual with my kids, I listen to their problems and together we explore ways to resolve them. In Salvador's case, the apparent problem was an estrangement from his older brother, caused by a personal slight: a year before, his brother had forgotten to pick him up from a friend's house. Now, unwilling to swallow his pride, Salvador not only missed the friendship of his brother but he also missed time spent with his four-year-old nephew, his brother's son. In ten minutes, I convinced him to go talk to his brother. He did, explaining his hurt feelings, and suddenly the two brothers were tight again.

The next time Salvador came to me for a heart-to-heart he seemed agitated and about to cry. He sat down at a table in the empty classroom and blurted out, "I've got a terrible problem with my brother, Mr. White. Really bad!"

"Tell me, Salvador, what is it?" I said, sensing I was to hear something terrible.

"He's gay," he said, lips trembling. "I just found out." Salvador then put his head on the table and sobbed away, chest heaving. I felt like laughing out loud but I held back. In Salvador's gang world the sense of manhood among abused, addicted, angry, and fatherless boys is so fragile and uncertain that anything they perceive as a threat to their veneer of machismo is terrifying to them.

Instead of laughing, I patted him on the shoulder. "Salvador," I said, "I've got good news for you. Homosexuality is not contagious. Not only that, but you're actually free to love and care about your brother. You can respect his right to make lifestyle choices, and you can disagree with his choices, just as he can disagree with yours." The crying soon stopped, and Salvador lifted his head and grew calm. He appeared to realize that he didn't have to fear, fight, or insult every person who was different from him. "Try talking to your brother," I said, "and let me know how it works out." He did and the whole family ended up embracing and growing closer than they were before.

I felt wonderful seeing such growth in Salvador. I was proud of him, which made his ultimate betrayal of my rules and trust in him that much more painful. For several months, he'd been driving a car to school without permission and, I discovered, had also been lying to me about having a driver's permit when he didn't. He also had bullied other kids into not telling me and even had mocked and assaulted another boy for cutting his gang ties. He got away with lying and driving around because no one called him on it, including his mother. Then he bragged about it at school to our security guard, and that's when I found out and confronted him. With a scared look in his eyes, Salvador admitted he'd been lying to me and I dropped him on the spot.

How critical is honesty and integrity to holding up the foundation of these kids' lives? Within two or three months of giving up on both those qualities, Salvador stopped going to school, dropped the auto mechanics class, lost his job, blew his bank account, was convicted of stealing a car, and was incarcerated in juvenile camp.

I blame myself partly because I didn't see the signs. I should have paid closer attention to him. As a reclamation project, he was like freshly poured concrete. He needed constant watching and shaping and I must have missed a sign or clue in his actions. The other part that explains his failure to stick to my rules is that he probably came to West Valley too late. His core had already hardened. On the surface he learned to be polite, attentive, and a steady worker at his part-time fast-food job. But under that shell of pretense, he remained a nasty character. He knew the rules perfectly and though he probably regretted betraying me, he was fully aware of what he was doing.

COMPASSION AT WORK

On one of our field trips to tour a university campus, I asked our tour guide, a bubbly blonde who was a fourth-year business and math major, if she could tell me and my students what her goals were. Without hesitating she replied, "Make money and travel." I nodded, she smiled, and then she added with a perky glance at the kids, "Entertain myself and make more money." I detected no awareness on her part that her future plans focused on anyone but herself. For their part, my students listened politely, probably thinking her response was normal and nothing they hadn't heard before. Later, I pointed out to them that our young guide had said nothing about wanting to help others. She didn't even hint at wishing to change the world.

"This is how you can come out ahead of these guys," I told my kids. "This is your leg up. After you go through the West Valley program, you're going to have something people want. That girl might be brilliant in math but she's illiterate in matters of the heart. You've got something she and others like her don't have. You can also get what she has, easier than she can get what you've got."

The Dalai Lama explains his compassion by simply saying that his religion is kindness, which could be seen as the flip side of the campus guide's mission in life. Fortunately, after we returned to West Valley, Nola provided the perfect contrast to selfish aims. Hardly a Buddhist, she was wearing her totems, the Tinker Bell and Raiders necklaces, when I asked her to tell us about her training as a nurse's assistant at a seniors convalescent home. Standing at the front of the room, Nola, the big girl with an easy smile, shyly described the drama of a recent day at work:

> There's this old man. He's paralyzed, can't move at all, though he smiles when he's awake. He has this G-tube we feed him through, both food and water. And he's got some

huge bedsores on his rear end. You can see right through to the bone. So yesterday I help a nurse get him off the bed with restraints so we could take him to the shower. We take off his diaper, then lift him up over the floor to put him down on the shower chair. All of a sudden he takes a dump, right there on the floor. Really awful but the poor guy had no control. So we set him down on the shower chair and roll him to the shower room. We clean him up with soapy water and then rinse him off. The whole time he's just staring straight ahead. We clean up his mess on the floor and after we put another diaper on him, we set him back in bed. . . . Down the hall I go into the room of another patient, an old lady who keeps saying, "Who's that man? Who's that man?" She keeps pointing at the window but when I look, nobody's there. "What man, which man?" I say. And she says, "That man." I don't know what to tell her but I say, "I don't see a man." Then she gets angry. "Go call my nurse!" she yells and starts cursing at me. So I press the nurse-call button by the bed and when the duty nurse comes, she says, "Oh, just come on outside and we'll talk to her. We'll calm her down." I step into the hallway and just then we hear the lady scream. When we go back in the room, there she is with blood all over the bed. She'd just pulled out one of her eyes and is holding it in her hand. I can't move. I stand there while the other nurses come and give her first aid. Then I help clean up the mess. The lady's wearing a patch and I'm told not to get too close to her. . . . I don't wear makeup anymore when I go to the place because I cry all the time. Every time I see the man with the bedsores I cry. And he's not the only one. The nurses are supposed to move them around every two hours so they won't get the sores, but they don't.

Nola trailed off and grew quiet, while her fellow students, some of them tearful, began to applaud. In Studs Terkel's 1972 bestseller *Working,* one of his interview subjects, in talking about her work, says, "I think most of us are looking for a calling, not a job. Most of us, like the assembly line worker, have jobs that are too small for our spirit. Jobs are not big enough for people." I believe Nola, who has her sights set on an RN degree, has found her calling.

Three months later, Nola graduated at the top of her nursing class, earning her licenses as a certified nursing assistant and a home health care aide. All her expenses were paid by Hope's Nest, a charity that also contributes to West Valley. Eighteen months after coming to West Valley, she also graduated from our program. Now, inspired by Nola's example, her old girlfriends who first enticed her away from school have reenrolled.

Recently, I saw Nola wearing a necklace. Fearing she was still sporting the Raiders medallion, I cried out, "Nola! What are you wearing?"

She pulled it out of her shirt to show me: the little green fairy with the magic wand.

"Don't worry, Mr. White," she said. "I'm just a Tinker Bell girl now."

STONE SOUP LESSON

One story I tell my students to show how hearts can change is a folktale about a poor village in Russia long ago. Wars had ravaged the land, nothing grew, and the villagers had nothing to eat. Everyone was holding on to the little bit of food each person had. One day two soldiers wandered into the village from the latest war. Desperately hungry, they begged for food, but no one would give them even a breadcrumb to eat. What could they do? After thinking awhile, the soldiers picked up a few stones and wrapped them in cloth. Then they asked one of the villagers if they could borrow a pot. Since the men weren't asking for food, the villager loaned them a pot.

The soldiers filled the pot with water from a stream, put the stones in, and built a fire to boil the water. Soon the villagers got curious and began coming out of their houses. "What are you doing?" someone asked.

"Oh, we're making stone soup for all of you," one of the soldiers answered. "We're going to share."

"I see," said one villager. "It'll probably be better with some onions. I've got some that I can put into your soup."

"I've got some carrots," said another villager.

"And I've got some potatoes," a third added.

Before long, everybody was tossing something into the pot. Soon they were all gathered around, filling their bowls. Everyone ate, everyone shared. There was plenty of stew to go around and the day ended happily for all.

In class we discuss the story and come up with the following moral or lesson: When the soldiers stopped asking for food and started offering to share, the villagers lost their fear of not having enough. They had a change of heart and suddenly everyone began to share and care for each other.

Whenever I can arrange to make such a lesson in sharing come alive for my students, when I can give them a chance to give as the villagers gave, I often hear grumbling. This happened among four West Valley girls when I asked if they were willing to give twelve inches of their hair to a group, called Locks of Love, that makes wigs for children with cancer who've gone bald as a result of chemotherapy treatments. Reluctantly, the girls gave up their hair, but not without audible complaints and whining.

"Girls," I told them, "don't focus on how short or long your hair is now. You have something today that you didn't have yesterday. To some degree you've found the reason why you're here—and I don't mean in this room. I mean on the planet. Somebody's life is better because of something you did. Somebody's going to cry a little less, smile a little more, because of some easy-to-do, cost-free, painless little thing you did. Every time you think of your new haircut, remember: yes, it changed your looks, but hair grows back. Don't obsess about it. Think of the children. Aren't you glad you did something that will make them feel good? I'm proud of you."

The grumbling died down and in time the Locks of Love girls' hair grew back, and they told me in different ways that they were proud of what they had done.

Schools and Parents

- You can repeat this and other stories with messages about people sharing and caring. However, there's no substitute for practicing compassion. The lessons and rewards of raising spirits by means of simple acts of kindness only make sense and stick if a child experiences them repeatedly.

Rule #9

WE LEARN FROM EVERYTHING

What brought me here was finding myself in the dean's office every morning. I was fighting and not paying attention. Now I have two jobs [and] a savings account, and I don't disrespect my mother. School is more fun and I'm learning.

—Monica, 14, West Valley student
who previously had chronic behavior problems

We learn from everything we experience in order to be independent, contributing people of integrity and good character. This is what I tell my students. I write "independent," "contributing," "integrity," and "good character" on the chalkboard. I tell them "independent" means "out on your own, able to support yourself." "Contributing" is when they "do something to make the world better, helping, caring about others." If they do these things, they will be people of "integrity" and "good character:" morally strong, honest, and compassionate human beings.

Having these qualities doesn't guarantee success in anything. "You also need history, English, math, science, economics, and government," I explain to newcomers. "If you stick with the program, you'll learn enough of these subjects to prepare you for what's ahead, enough to get you started. I don't want you sitting here too long." I add that if they're behind with their credits they can expect to catch up, either by working toward completing their credits or by passing a proficiency test for a high school diploma, whichever is quickest. At the same time, they'll be either taking a community college class or attending a vocational class. It's their choice. But by the time they leave West Valley they should know whether to pursue a college degree or learn a trade.

Whatever career preparation they choose, academic or vocational training, they should have what it takes to live on their own. "No guarantees," I say, "but just by being here, even if it's only for a day, the school's already affected you. You're headed in the right direction."

By "direction" I don't mean a specific profession such as astronaut or auto mechanic. It's not what or where they're headed to that's important; it's how they're going about it, and the fact that they are headed somewhere positive. Is it with integrity or without? They once came to me as rejects because they were forever making bad decisions. I just want them to leave the school with a foundation of values for making good decisions. That's my definition of success. It's not the job, profession, or income level they reach that's of primary importance. It's whether or not they become hardworking men and women of good character.

NO FRICTION WHEN YOU FOLLOW THE RULES

We begin every morning with a "patriotic exercise," as required by state law but largely ignored by most secondary schools. We stand and either we recite the Pledge of Allegiance or I read briefly from such documents as the U.S. Constitution, the Declaration of Independence, or the Gettysburg Address. After this, we have a five-minute silent "meditation time." This is followed by a brief "morning meeting," when I go over what we'll be doing for the rest of the day. Included in the morning meeting are my quick, doctor-like "rounds" among the students. I check with each of them on the status of whatever was pending in their lives when we finished up on the previous school day. *Maria, did you pass your driver's ed test? Luis, how's that job switch? Did you talk to your boss? Angie, how're you handling the boyfriend thing? Is he still in jail? Salvador, did you get that ingrown toenail taken care of? Guys, you've got to act on these things. You can't let them fester. They'll only get worse.*

The rounds are part drum beating and part status checkup. It's early and I want their attention, but I also want to know what's going on in their personal lives. I believe there must be some sort of soul-deep connection between a teacher and student before any real learning can take place. I'm as committed to and concerned about them as I would be if they were my own kids; I do for them what I'd do for my own kids if my wife and I had chosen to have children. Certainly I spend many more quality hours with them each day than their parents do—roughly from 8:30 A.M. to 3:30 P.M.—talking, listening, observing, noticing. And then, of course, there are the after-school phone calls from individual students. These come in until about 10 P.M. or later and start up the next morning at 6.

I approach everything as part of an organic whole. Last night's shift at McDonald's, a fight with a younger sister, serving food at a homeless shelter, or helping pitch tents on a class camping trip is just as relevant as every lesson, every exercise, every essay, every math problem, and every reading assignment. Everything they learn and do is connected, which is why I do the rounds before starting the day's lessons. I hear what they've been doing, what problems they're facing since I last saw them. Everyone hears. Together we sometimes thrash out a kid's crisis. *Jimmy ran from a gang, jumped over a fence, and got away. How many of you have been chased by a gang? Come on, hands. Were you afraid?* We talk about courage, about fear. We get things out. *Graciela, why so sad today? Don't tell me it's that boyfriend again? What did he do this time? You dumped him? Good!*

After we clear the air of personal problems and understand the real and selfless purpose of why we're learning, increasing the students' academic knowledge practically takes place automatically. *Okay, current events. Newspapers—Alice, Nola, pass them out. . . . Read the headlines, front page. Find the word that means the same thing as standing up to someone face-to-face. "Grapple"? No, that might come afterward. "Confronts," right!* First we tackle vocabulary through the newspaper headlines, page by page. Then we discuss the consequences of certain events, frequently relating them to other course work. For example, we calculate how much each of the ten jetliners China ordered from Boeing will cost and how many more workers will be employed, families supported, taxes collected, schools and stores affected. It's an exercise in math, economics, and sociology.

Next, we move to our history textbooks. The pace is brisk but we slow down if something important rivets our attention. Soon we're reviewing the chapter on the war in Vietnam. *Remember, big picture first—main players, main issues, important dates.* We look at the wall map of the world, locate Vietnam and its neighbors. "Why do we have wars?" asks Melissa, a thirteen-year-old middle school dropout and victim of too many fights with gang girls. Her question, which I pose to the class, spawns a discussion of global economics in which we define terms such as "spheres of influence" and "domino effect." I don't belabor the facts, but I want them to know about President Johnson, the Demilitarized Zone, napalm, the North Vietnamese, My Lai, communism, and capitalism. Sometimes we slide over to related topics, such as Melissa's grandfather, a Marine who was wounded in the war and now walks with a limp, or the Vietnamese refugees who came to the United States after the war.

We spend most of our time in one room, but we also use the adjacent computer room or the parents' meeting room, where we keep microscopes and art supplies. Sonny Poremba, a substitute teacher and artist, painted the walls surrounding the computers with reproductions of classic artworks and styles, from prehistoric cave paintings of bison to Mayan figurines to the Mona Lisa, Dalí's droopy watches, and Picasso's self-portrait. Sonny also painted the walls of the meeting room with twenty-two animals and insects in a tropical setting, including a life-size Asian elephant. A twenty-third creature lurks somewhere in the foliage of our "jungle room," giving new students a *Where's Waldo?* challenge to find the critter. Every day these additions to the school enfold us in color and whimsy—and also help me illustrate art and biology lessons.

On another day during our history lesson, we go over the book's brief description of Cambodian leader Pol Pot and the meaning of words such as "genocide," "holocaust," and "ethnic cleansing." The next day we watch the film *The Killing Fields*, and this story later connects with a visit by an Auschwitz survivor, Eva Brown, who wants to share her experience with West Valley students. Her story and the numbers tattooed on her forearm hold their attention so strongly that they forget about themselves for a while. Morality, right and wrong, conscience, forgiveness—for the moment these become *living* concepts. My younger kids, aged thirteen and fourteen, are just as engaged as the older teenagers. In questions of character and human values, they don't have to be smarter, older, or quicker to grasp the meaning of evil.

My students wrote letters of appreciation to Mrs. Brown, as they do for all special visitors to the school. Here are excerpts of a few composed on their school computers, the first by a seventeen-year-old boy and the second and third by sixteen-year-old girls:

> I used to be a really bad guy and I used to believe in the things that got sixty of your family members killed. I

thought I was a neo-Nazi, but now I have changed. I can see past the color of someone's skin or what they believe in. . . . I used to think that certain groups of people were the cause of today's messed up society but it doesn't mean that all the people from that group are bad. They could be some of the kindest people in the world. . . . Please forgive me for all the times I disrespected your people by calling them names. I thought that all the pain and suffering they were put through was a joke, but it's not. . . . You said if you don't forgive, you will live in anger and unhappiness. You have to be a bigger person and step up and forgive. I learned to forgive from you. Thank you.

I was sorry to hear about your family but I can't understand how you could forgive. To be honest with you I am pretty sure that you loved them all very much just like I love my family and if somebody would ever harm them, I wouldn't be able to say that I forgive them. I feel that I would hate them for the rest of my life. . . . I seriously admire you because you just have a big heart after all the bad things that happened to you. . . . Your story really changed my way of thinking. I feel different in a good way and I am telling you I'm in the process of becoming a better person. I am going to forgive everybody that has hurt me and I am going to say sorry to the people who I think I have hurt. Once again, thank you for opening my eyes towards hate and about how much it's going to hurt me if I continue with hatred in my heart. Take good care of your lovely self.

I learned a lot about the Holocaust. I never knew that Jews suffered so much. . . . You did many crazy things to survive. You pretended acting like you knew how to play the flute just for a loaf of bread; risking your life. You tied a rag around your leg to stop the bleeding after a dog bit you, and nothing happened to you. It was a real miracle not getting any type of disease on your leg. . . . I thought Mexicans had it bad by trying to cross the border. You on the other hand walked a death walk for two weeks with no food or water. You had to drink your own urine to survive that walk. I'm really sorry for all that you went through and for losing all those family members. . . . I really admire all you did. You're my hero.

When all the rules are followed, from showing up and telling the truth to caring for others, an entire classroom of difficult children is transformed and miracles happen, like Eva Brown's changing the heart of a neo-Nazi gang kid. Again, the key is to have everyone following the rules. So whatever the subject or topic, everything in class hums. Distractions bounce off, eyes focus, hands are raised, voices seldom rise. It's a teacher's dream—a place that's clean, safe, and intellectually real. There's no friction, no resistance, no difference between how they should act and how they do act. All of them manage to keep up and no one gets left behind. Even Ernie, the slow-moving, big kid who had fogged his brain with pot for three years, contributes to the discussion. When I mention the different faces of evil, he particularly condemns marijuana.

TEACHERS ARE OVERWHELMED

So many teachers today are so overwhelmed with state-mandated achievement measurements and other demands that such topics as honesty, courage, compassion, and other moral virtues are seen as trivial time wasters. This obsession with testable standards reaches its most dangerous extreme with algebra hysteria. In many school districts if students don't pass this subject, they don't graduate; often, discouraged and disheartened, they drop out of school.

I teach algebra and make sure they're skilled enough to pass certain proficiency tests. However, I believe algebra is given far too much importance as a graduation requirement and its real-world relevance is greatly overrated. Yes, basic algebra, geometry, math, and other problem-solving skills are important and must be learned. But I object to achieving this goal in a way that destroys the self-confidence and future of countless capable and otherwise intelligent kids. It's like requiring all prospective graduates to run a mile under six minutes or draw a beautiful picture, regardless of their aptitudes for running or drawing. Algebra is only one of many measures of intelligence and good judgment, and we can't just lump all kids together in a one-size-fits-all approach. I believe the almost hateful insistence on not giving diplomas to children who can't pass algebra has come about mostly because education leaders are so bent on appearing strong and on climbing up the promotional ladder that they don't mind crushing children under unrealistic requirements.

Using my rules, all schools, big as well as small, can accomplish what I believe are the educational system's two main goals: teach children the academic skills they'll need to perform twenty-first-century tasks, and at the same time teach them that the primary value of academic knowledge is to enable us to uplift, heal, inspire, and bring about the progress of all mankind. As I have seen for twenty-five years and continue to see in class every day, this kind of curriculum emphasis brings measurable results that verge on the incredible.

At the Mid-Valley Community Day school where I taught in San Diego County, in one year I took the scores of Indian and Mexican children who had never done well and brought their tested learning levels to historical highs. As an administrator, I didn't do anything out of the ordinary in the classrooms. Though it may sound simplistic and saccharine, their academic growth spurt was mainly a side effect of knowing that their principal loved them, valued them, and would do anything to help them.

At another school, a charter-school in San Luis Obispo, I took a modestly performing group of affluent white children and produced an average academic growth of two years in all subjects for the entire school in *eight months*. Sure, they worked hard and creatively on their studies, but the big learning jump was solely the inevitable side effect of showing them how exciting it was to exercise their compassion and caring instincts. Among the projects they took on: communicating directly with Pierre Byoya, the leader of Burundi, to try and figure out a way to bring peace to that East African hot spot, and growing food for the homeless.

At West Valley, my mostly low-income, urban students don't "catch up" to students in traditional public schools; they far exceed them. I've had many come to me as fifteen-year-old semiliterates and eventually graduate from West Valley ahead of their age group and move on to college.

No matter where or with whom my rules have been applied, they reveal the universal truth that academic growth is not cause but effect, the result of young minds and hearts wanting to do good as men and women of character and moral courage. Schools that follow my rules won't have to exchange "smart" kids for "good" kids. They won't have to come up with excuses for why their children are "really nice" but are not doing well on their testing. That's because every student will behave well and perform well academically. The only catch is that these schools must first insist that every student and parent involved in the school follow the rules.

None of our top national problems, from corporate graft and environmental abuse to racism, drugs, and the crumbling sense of family were caused by our inability to manipulate a variable or graph the slope of a line with algebraic equations. For the most part the cause of these problems lies in failing to raise children to be men and women of moral courage and integrity. Moral, not academic, illiteracy is the greatest threat to our future.

PROBLEMS BEGIN AT HOME

Most serious problems of character and integrity begin at home, and parents of delinquents share much of the blame for their children's misbehavior. Schools then are left with the fallout of poor parenting and must scramble to patch up the damage already done. If the school your child attends has no interest in considering my rules and you want to adopt some or all on your own, start with the ones that make the most sense to you. Set up a zero-tolerance and reward system. Violations bring the removal of privileges: car use, allowance, extended curfews, and other perks of good behavior. Compliance, on the other hand, produces added privileges—not only material rewards, which often send the wrong message, but more choices and responsibilities.

Committed parents should start a weekly progress plan with their children in which they set specific goals and the time needed to achieve them. Every week my students fill out a form listing school, home, and personal-problem goals, for example, "I will wash the dinner dishes every night without being told. I will not drink beer this week. Or I will not shout at or argue with anyone at school all week." Review the plan and take each item seriously. Everything is fair game as a goal, from a chore to a daily geometry homework lesson. No matter how trivial the goal seems, it should be considered an important character builder.

As for nightly homework, the way it is assigned in traditional schools makes it counterproductive. Of course, children should have work to do after school. My students certainly do. They have to take a college or vocational class of their choosing and they have to work part-time jobs. They can also take art, karate, or piano lessons, which we pay for. They're encouraged to get involved in counseling or religious activities, and they have to help out at home.

To have children grind out seven hours of academic classes and then send them home with more repetitive make-work assignments creates an imbalance in their lives and character. This does nothing but encourage many of them to cheat and hate learning. On the other hand, by arranging our school day the way I've described, my students show up an hour or more before they have to, frequently stay with me voluntarily for two or three hours after the class day is over, and say that they feel our school is like a second home.

ONE BOY FINDS INTEGRITY

If at some point during the day's lessons someone in my class gets stuck in a learning rut, I tell him or her that I'll help them out after I dismiss class for the day. In this way I was able to help a boy who came to West Valley during the spring as a sixteen-year-old junior from a nearby traditional high school. He seldom attended and was such a poor student that he had fallen hopelessly behind. This boy was large, 6'2" and 250 pounds, and he'd always wanted to play football, but he never had been able to because of his poor grades. On his own initiative he came to us and asked to be admitted. I told him that if he followed our rules and focused on catching up, I was sure he could make up his credits and return in the fall to his old school and the football program.

Fully motivated, he kept to the rules: he showed up every

day, got a job as a grocery checker, and started taking an automotive mechanics class at an occupational center. For a guy who could bench-press three hundred pounds and wanted to smash other players, he was an amazingly gentle and honest soul. He struggled with most assignments, but math was his undoing. When he arrived at West Valley, he tested years below grade level in his ability with numbers.

Throughout his time with me, whenever I thought his efforts in class were flagging, I'd remind him that he didn't start out bench-pressing three hundred pounds. He started at less than two hundred and worked his way up. It didn't happen overnight and there was no need to get down on himself. With time he would solve the equation. "Try," I said one afternoon after class let out. "Break this problem down into small steps, just like we did in class with the other problems."

He hunched over the sheet of paper and puzzled over the last of three algebraic equations. He'd finished the first two during class. Five minutes, ten minutes, fifteen minutes passed. Suddenly he shouted, "I did it! Mr. White, I did it!"

I walked over to his table where he was grinning and holding the paper in the air like a trophy. "All right, big guy," I said. "Let's have a look." I saw that he'd done it correctly and patted him on the back. "See you tomorrow," I told him.

We operate the school year-round and require concurrent vocational or college classes, and this boy studied diligently through the summer and made up a year's work in little more than half a year. He transferred back to his original school, made the varsity football team, subsequently starred as a defensive lineman, made the league all-star team, and has offers to play in college. His regeneration required enormous courage and persistence, and the payoff was more than a season of spectacular tackles or a high school diploma. He gained something intangible and priceless: integrity.

WE NEED TO CHANGE HOW WE TEACH

As a teacher, I do what teachers traditionally do and what the law requires: I create lessons and teach to specific objectives, test my students, mark papers, give grades, catch their mistakes, have them rewrite papers, redo math problems, record results, and measure progress. In addition, educational codes throughout the country require teachers to pay attention to character values, generally a fuzzy area many educators ignore. I don't. In fact, section 233.5 (a) of California's education code forms the basis for my approach to teaching:

> Each teacher shall endeavor to impress upon the minds of the pupils the principles of morality, truth, justice, patriotism, and a true comprehension of the rights, duties, dignity of American citizenship, and the meaning of equality and human dignity.

These are more than mere words; they're ideals. I have a poster of these words hanging on the wall at the front of the class for a reason. They serve as beacons or mental checks whenever I think we need it, which is every day. Sometimes we read them as the morning's patriotic exercise or we discuss the meaning of a particular word. For instance, Eva Brown put flesh on the word "dignity" and removed it from the realm of abstract ideas when she described how the Nazis tried to take her dignity away in the concentration camp.

For the kids, listening to a sprightly Holocaust survivor describe naked humiliation was an exercise in feeling empathy. She explained how it felt to her as a girl and that somehow she kept her courage and sense of self-worth. When my students understand the meaning of dignity in this way, the lesson goes deep. It affects character and stays in the memory, which is the best kind of learning.

We must change the public school system; too many young lives across America are being lost. Juvenile delinquents end up in what I call without much exaggeration, gangster day-care centers euphemistically called "alternative" schools. The better-behaved kids—which means most of them—aren't much better off in traditional public schools. They're also generally warehoused on sprawling, sterile campuses where they're forced to create mutant social groups to escape the loneliness of anonymity. Too often these students, lacking a sense of purpose, warm seats and mark time until they graduate with a one-dimensional view of life limited to college, careers, marriages, kids, divorces, old age, and their ultimate demise. And we wonder why so many kids have no interest in school.

It's as if the obesity epidemic among our children is ironically reflecting their inability to satisfy their real hunger for a life view that is more soul-fulfilling than the spiritually empty curriculum we're currently offering them. Common sense says that school leaders must institute a values-driven curriculum that doesn't just teach children how to exist but also gives them a reason for living. We need a curriculum that emphasizes integrity, moral courage, compassion, selfless service to others, and respect for the law. These principles and goals are actually supported in many education codes, but educators too often refuse to apply what the law provides for.

TEACHING ACADEMICS IS NOT THE PROBLEM

Again, content, or the academic subjects students learn, is not the main problem in our schools. We may be good at teaching kids skills for staying alive, but we haven't been nearly so good at teaching them what they're living for. We must give them a life-affirming purpose to live for; once we do that, learning will flourish. As I've shown in earlier chapters, some values and qualities, such as compassion and mental toughness, can be taught and practiced.

Years ago, I began to develop my rules when I began teaching the worst kids at Cave and Cooper elementary schools in Vallejo. At Cooper I was known as a disciplinarian. Ellen Nims, the principal, even told me, "It takes a tough teacher to teach tough kids." She explained that toughness helps keep order but it wasn't the main reason she hired me for my first full-time job in the classroom. She said she'd always been good at spotting which teachers would always put the children first in their professional and even private lives. She sensed I had such a quality, which she referred to as "a heart for kids."

Eventually she taught me a lot about teaching, but more important, she supported my methods. I emphasized values and discipline before academic achievement, for once these are in place, learning inevitably rises to high levels. Improved grades and test scores became the result, or effect, of preparing students with a reliable foundation of values.

Peter, my little ball of fighting fury at Cooper who just wanted to be left alone, was one of my first challenges and successes—once I made him my special project. Peter was only one student, but I thought I could duplicate my approach with an entire class of delinquents. I believed the principle at work was the same for one as it was for many. Get students to like going to class and attendance zooms upward.

I had lost touch with Peter several years after he moved up to higher grades. But over the years I often wondered what had happened to him. What kind of a man had he become? Had my rules taken hold? Curious, I wanted to find out. Visiting Vallejo some years ago and remembering the way to his parents' home, I knocked on the front door. Peter's mother answered and immediately recognized me. She welcomed me warmly and invited me in. Peter, she said, would be home in a few minutes from his construction job.

While I waited, I admired a picture on the mantle of his daughter, a little girl in a softball uniform. She wasn't much younger than Peter was when I was his teacher. As predicted, about then Peter pulled up into the driveway in his car. When he got out, I could see he was now a big, muscular young man. Entering the house, he stopped short when he saw me sitting in the living room, perhaps mistaking me for a cop. I stood up and said with a mock serious expression, "I came to check your homework. It had better be done." After an uncomprehending frozen moment, he suddenly grinned. "Mr. White!" he said, and then walked over to me and we hugged.

We reminisced about our days together at Cooper School and how his life had changed. Peter had skipped a grade and caught up to his peers, joining the sixth-graders. Eventually, he passed into middle school and then high school. As happens to many kids in their early school years, Peter's inability to succeed academically had taken away any joy he might have gotten from school. The result was that he had stayed home from school as much as possible and constantly misbehaved when he did attend. It had taken special care to help him break the cycle of failure he'd known until then. Improved reading skill brought its own rewards of pride and growing self-esteem, and regular attendance had soon become the inevitable side effect.

Looking back on how I got Peter on track, I'm convinced it was his innate toughness that I built on. I believe as a boy he respected me because he sensed that I had that same quality; he disdained people he felt talked tough but had nothing to back it up. As his teacher so many years ago, I realize how mental toughness and a strong work ethic are still critical to overcoming problems and finding success. For Peter, now a committed father with a steady job, toughness paid off.

Schools

- Begin a values-driven curriculum that emphasizes integrity, moral courage, and respect for the law.
- Enforce the rules with strong security and expulsion measures.

- Make sure the school is a safe, secure environment for students to learn free of violence and fear.

Parents

- Make your home a learning environment.
- Support such changes at your child's school by following my rules at home, if not all the way at first, then in incremental stages.
- Look at yourselves first. If your children are ill behaved and problematic at school, you must shoulder considerable blame for this, since most serious problems of character and integrity begin at home.

Rule #10

WE MAKE A DIFFERENCE

Before I came here I almost never went to school and I got straight F's. Now I have one hundred percent attendance, good grades, a job, savings, and I'm interested in my future. Being at West Valley helped me learn that I can do anything I put my mind to.

—James, 15, West Valley student; former dropout

The changes we make in our lives make a tangible, often powerful, difference in the lives of others. I make a difference when I coach my students away from gangs, drugs, and lying. They make a difference when they land good jobs because they're polite, prepared, and presentable. Together we make a difference in our homes and communities just by being respectful, law-abiding citizens. Better yet, we make a huge difference when we see a wrong committed and have the moral courage to stand up for what's right.

Eva Brown gave me a framed statement attributed to Martin

Niemoller, a German Lutheran pastor who opposed the Nazis. It hangs in our main classroom like a beacon of truth, a reminder of the consequences of turning our backs on evil. This is a variant found on most American and English posters.

> First . . . they came for the socialists, and I did not speak up because I was not a socialist. Then they came for the trade unionists, and I did not speak up because I was not a trade unionist. Then they came for the Jews, and I did not speak up because I was not a Jew. Then they came for me, and there was no one left to speak up for me.

The lesson here for all of us is obvious. My students, most of whom come from poor families, describe how evil prospers where they live and what happens when no one has the courage to speak out: armed criminals take over, normal folks hide in their homes, and everyone is scared into silence by the gangs.

CLEANING UP THE AREA

Before we opened West Valley, in 2000, drug dealers, pimps, prostitutes, gangbangers, and other criminal characters were gaining an increasingly high profile in the surrounding streets. My fellow teacher Bob McGill and I looked at our situation in this area, the western part of San Fernando Valley, and didn't like what we saw. Too many kids joined gangs, drug abuse was a scourge, and violent incidents were commonplace. We saw what this was doing to a community of working-class people and we wanted to do something about it.

With the financial and supervisory support of the Los Angeles County Office of Education, Bob and I moved from the Mid-Valley school in Van Nuys to begin our ideal alternative program. Like other community day schools, it targeted delinquent teenagers who have exhausted all other nontraditional school options. However, I would run West Valley Leadership Academy in Canoga Park by my rules and as a one-class school. We fine-tuned certain methods and practices, focusing on students' individual personalities and progress instead of their past misdeeds and gang affiliation. For the first time I had the freedom to operate a school as I saw fit. Our enrollment numbers were small, typically about thirty, but I had already shown at larger schools that an enforceable, values-centered approach worked just as well in a large school as in a small one. The principle was the same.

We opened our school in a vacant two-story office building at the locus of the typical Los Angeles dichotomy. In one direction were pockets of lovely estate homes, and in many other directions people were shooting up heroin in nearby alleys. All things illegal were openly bought and sold on the streets, and gangsters brazenly controlled a growing number of neighborhoods. Several blocks from the school a gas station sold crack pipes disguised as little flower vases. Down the street a gang-run tattoo parlor, two head shops, a liquor store that sold alcohol and drugs to kids, and a drug-dealing strip joint thrived. My students couldn't walk to school without weaving through dozens and dozens of idle homeless men and illegal itinerant Mexican day laborers harassing them with looks and words. We complained to the police, but they did little more than drive by the sidewalk carnival of criminals and other lowlifes from time to time.

Finally, Bob and I decided to take these people on by our-selves. One by one, we began to confront them. In the tattoo shop the gangster owner and I screamed at each other for almost an hour, going toe-to-toe over their harassment of passersby and other suspicious activities. We complained to the head office of the gas station selling the crack pipes. We gave the police depart-ment deadlines for taking long overdue law-enforcement action or threatened to hold press conferences on the street corner for TV and print reporters, pointing out the dealers and others traf-ficking in drugs, sex, and illegal weapons. We planned to com-plain in front of TV cameras that the cops were not responding.

It took months of such activity—a combination of press at-tention to the situation and police surveillance—finally to get most of the druggies and other predators to leave the area. We helped close down three crack houses in the neighborhood around the school, confronted the owner of a liquor store that sold drugs to kids, and chased away a dealer of false IDs. We also harassed the daylights out of the guy who owned (and still owns) the strip club down the street, two drug paraphernalia shops, and the previously mentioned tattoo parlor. The strip-club people re-placed their sign with one that was more discreet, the gang mem-bers who frequented the tattoo parlor stopped loitering outside, the gas station stopped selling crack pipes, and we put the drug paraphernalia shops on notice to operate within the law.

We went outside the school to help clean up the neighbor-hood because we wanted to keep the streets safe for our stu-dents. We challenged the bad guys because we saw these students as our own children. What we were doing was no different from what any concerned parent would do to protect their children.

As for the actual parents of these kids, most of them were hard pressed to help us. For the most part they were and are overburdened by work demands, are frightened of the gangs, or are complacent about or unaware of the evils surrounding their children. In many cases, Mom and Dad abused alcohol at home and in a few others they even used and sold drugs themselves.

For practical purposes, parents and educators have to accept the fact that the need for effective parenting and teaching never really ends, especially the sacrifice it often takes to be a good role model. Without this ongoing willingness to sacrifice time, money, personal convenience, and, sometimes, personal safety, good parenting and teaching cannot be achieved.

It is not today's kids who have changed. They're no different than kids have ever been: innately selfish, trying every possible way to evade responsibility and the necessity of growing up, not knowing where the boundaries of acceptable behavior really are, and desperately looking to parents and teachers to show them. No, kids haven't changed; the parents and teachers have changed. Too often they have confused relating to children with acting like children.

These parents and teachers originally sign on for jobs whose primary prerequisites are unselfishness and the willingness to sacrifice personal comfort. Later, they realize this price is more than they're willing to pay. By this time it's too late to reverse course because parents can't evade their legal responsibility for their children and many teachers can't or don't want to change to another career outside of education. Now that we have too many parents and teachers like these, our homes and schools are suffering. Yet both institutions, in looking for solutions, are substituting money for morals, indulgence for instruction, and self-gratification for selflessness. Obviously, such fixes are not working.

VOICES FROM THE PAST AND ELSEWHERE

I don't claim that my rules are the only solution to our growing problems, but I do know that my way works. This is confirmed every day I'm in class and every time I hear from former students and visitors and from the messages I get from others about what goes on at West Valley. For example, Carlos, the Brando-Godfather impersonator from my Mid-Valley time, called recently to catch up on things—never mind that it was my statement to the court about his gang activity that helped put him in a youth prison. He knows he did some awful things and deserved punishment.

One episode in his life that I haven't mentioned occurred when he was twelve. The police had picked him up to pump him for information about his gang. Because he wouldn't inform on his fellow gang members, the police dropped him off in the neighborhood of a rival gang, announcing his presence on a loudspeaker. As soon as the cops pushed him out onto enemy turf and left the scene, the rival gangbangers closed in and beat him senseless.

Years later, he called to shoot the breeze and tell me he'd left Los Angeles and severed all his former gang ties. He had moved to the Midwest. "I like it here," he said excitedly. "People are so nice to me." There wasn't a hint of recrimination in his voice—in fact, just the opposite. He thanked me for keeping him out of further trouble, adding that he'd probably still be in prison if I hadn't stood up to him. We agreed nobody else would stand up to him.

"That hasn't changed," I complained. "Most of the city won't stand up to these gang kids. I think we've totally lost our courage." I refer to most gang members as "tofu" because I've seen statistics showing that more than three-fourths of them are not hard-core committed members but are lost, looking for somewhere to belong, and just take on the flavor of what's around them. With the right method, it's relatively easy to turn them around and get them out of the gang life. Carlos agreed, even though he had to travel halfway across the country to find a new life. He had done the right thing and made a difference for the future of himself and his wife.

Three people who've seen my work up close and personal provided me with their candid views of my approach to teaching for this book: a former Mid-Valley and West Valley student, Anthony de la Torre; the substance-abuse counselor Andrew Heiger; and the former Cooper Elementary School principal Ellen Nims. They present different perspectives on how, what, and why I do what I do.

West Valley is a beautiful school compared to Mid-Valley, which was a beat-up, crummy school—dirty, graffiti, gangs, fights in class. Mr. White pulled money out of his own pocket to fix it up. He painted the carpet, chairs, and most of the school. He challenged us to come to school every day for two months, and he'd get us caught up enough so we could transfer back to a regular school. I did. Compared to all the other teachers I've had, he's one of the best.

He'll sit you down and work with you. Other teachers would make us feel dumb. He would treat you as a person.

When I first saw him at Mid-Valley, I thought, who's this guy? He wants to make all these changes. I just wasn't ready for that life. But as I moved on, I look back at people like Mr. White who tried to help me and I'm sorry I didn't take that opportunity they gave me. It took me awhile to realize that.

I'm still in touch with him because I remember the good stuff he tried to do for me. He offered me his home, offered me money. He gave me money to buy clothes so I wouldn't get arrested for dressing all baggy. He kept me from violating my probation, bought me clothes to look for a job. He just put out a lot for me.

He thinks of his students as his own children. And that's very rare, especially for a bunch of kids just getting out of jail. Most people on the outside look at these kids as no good. I guess Paul White sees that these people have a soul and heart. He wants to give them the chances any other kid will get.

—Anthony de la Torre,
former Mid-Valley and West Valley student

I've known Paul White for at least six years. He brought some of his students to where I worked to have them tested for drugs [and] told me about his school, and I visited it. I talked to the students. I just loved the environment there. I went there to speak and asked if I could come by every week. I was going to fourteen different high schools a week and this school was definitely the most innovative and unique. His approach and the environment he created for the kids, his expectations of them, the way he talked to them, was genuine. He held them responsible for whatever they did, good and bad. He always praised them when they were doing good, and when they weren't, he would ask them, "What are you learning from that?" or "What's that going to get you?"

He's a great example of what these kids need. He's a teacher, sometimes a friend, sometimes a father. He is always consistent and very innovative with his thinking. A bum could be walking down the street and he'll say, "Hey, come in and talk to my kids." And he'll give the guy lunch in exchange for an hour of his time. He's able to convince a bum walking down the street to tell his story.

He has these teachable moments and turns them into something the kids don't forget. Even if the kids don't last at his school or they mess up or don't graduate, they'll keep in contact with him because he's the sort of guy you keep for life.

He's very approachable but holds them accountable. He's the first one to cheer them on when they do good and he's the first to take them aside when they're doing wrong and tell them, "Hey, knucklehead, what are you doing?" Kids need that. They run to it. It's a great thing he's got there. It's just common sense.

—Andrew Heiger, substance-abuse counselor

Twenty-something years ago, I hired Paul White because I instinctively felt a connection with him. I strongly sensed that he really cared about kids, was hardworking, and had high expectations for himself. I also felt he had the courage of his convictions.

In the 1980s teachers were still pretty much isolated in their classrooms with little or no collaborative opportunities. They were the masters of their domain, and most classrooms were highly teacher-centered. Most of my teachers did an excellent job of delivering the skills and knowledge needed for their grade levels. But increasingly, more high-risk students were coming to our school.

What I saw in Paul was the strong likelihood that his classroom would be student-centered, one in which he would look at each student as his job to reach and teach. For some of our students school was the only real constant in their life, and if a teacher shows that he cares, then he can build a strong connection with the student. Simply put, Paul cared.

During his first year at Cooper he developed strong relationships with the parents, especially those of the students exposed to risk factors which working together might reduce. There were parents who loved him one day and hated him the next because he had come down hard on them for lack of some responsibility or other. Nevertheless, these relationships remained strong, with the students most often the biggest beneficiaries of them.

He had high expectations for student behaviors and those with the most intensive needs received the closest level of monitoring. He also tried to involve the community in his students' growth and learning as much as possible. Several nursing homes were in walking distance, and his students would often visit them, present school-made gifts and cards, and perform musically during holidays. They had field trips all over the city, planted trees for the school, and invited speakers to the classroom. Although the phrase was not prevalent back then, Paul behaved as if it did take a village to raise a child, and if that [was] not always possible he would often try to be the village himself.

Today, more than twenty years later, I would not expect anything other than the success Paul has with students who are exposed to such significant handicaps that society has given up on them. School may be the only place that provides the structure, food, shelter, and protection for his students. He has made it his mission to make sure that, in fact, it does.

—Ellen Nims, Cooper Elementary School principal

KNOWING RIGHT FROM WRONG

From the outset I made sure that parents participated in our values-based approach to teaching their children. Everyone had to sign on to my rules, especially the one about at least trying to distinguish right from wrong. In our meetings and one-on-one conferences, I would tell parents my own Ventura story.

When I taught incarcerated teenagers in Ventura County youth jails, I had one very popular class that was called Men's Issues. The classroom was filled. Most of the guys were gang members who would show up voluntarily to hear me talk about how to become good men. One day an administrator in the program dropped by and asked me, "Why is this class so successful?"

"I talk to them," I said. "I tell them what's right."

He looked at me with the most perplexed expression, and then he asked, "Well, how *do* you know what's right?"

"How do you *not* know?" I said. "Human civilization didn't begin with just you and me. Most of the time it's easy to know what's right. Honesty is right, dishonesty is not. Moral courage is right, and self-interest and cowardice are not. Unselfishness and generosity are right and selfishness is wrong."

He still looked puzzled, not quite understanding, so I added a few more wrongs for good measure: "Racist behavior is wrong, gang activities are wrong, taking drugs is wrong, being lazy is wrong. How difficult is that?" He nodded and his flummoxed expression now had a touch of annoyance. I had just served up a tidy list of behaviors to look out for, and I don't think he had ever seen the lives of jailed kids reduced to such simple realities. When he left, I still didn't know if I had made sense to him. The same person was later part of an administrative group involved in a fiscal mismanagement scandal and lawsuit that cost the county schools millions of dollars in fines and settlements. This is what can happen when a person grows up without having a clear sense of what is right and what is not.

It's tragic. Educators know that every figure of strong moral character who has ever lived knew the basics of right from wrong. Religious leaders and others, they all followed certain absolute standards or beliefs as behavior guides. Whether we're religious or not, as parents and teachers I believe we have to instill some set of universal moral values in our children in order to help them recognize right from wrong. It's not that difficult if we have a moral compass or code of values ourselves.

But that's the catch. Many Americans have taken the discussion of faith-based values and moral absolutes out of our classrooms. In their pursuit of a standards-based education and their obsession with test scores and academic achievement, many school leaders have forgotten about behavior guides that used to be the lifeblood of American education. Manners, honesty, kindness, courage, and other virtues need to be taught in school, especially if children don't receive this kind of instruction at home. If we are to make a positive difference in life, we need such guides and virtues.

NO CHILD LEFT BEHIND?

Educators may have reasonable excuses for falling short of the "No Child Left Behind" mandates, but parents have no excuse for not teaching morality. Either they teach and enforce a set of values based on the concept of right and wrong, or they don't. If kids go off the rails at school, the first round of blame rests with their parents. At West Valley, I pound away at parents, promoting practical values and a commonsense nose for doing the right thing. At times I feel as if I have the smallest of fingers in the dike, but I remind them that they can still make a big difference in the lives of their teenagers. "It's not too late," I say, "but you've got to stay on them every day."

Parents can help matters by joining forces with teachers. For example, if a kid insists on doing something that will change his or her life for the better, we need to avoid the cookie-cutter view of students and look at what's best for them on a case-by-case basis. When one boy asks to take a noontime modern-dance class at the local community college, we talk it over. I see that it would mean the world to him, yet the class is held only at noon. No problem; he can leave the school for the class. But I warn him that if I catch him skipping dance and playing the Xbox at home, I'll yank him back to class for the full day. His mother agrees to be my ears and eyes in the home.

Another student takes a midday auto mechanics class at the occupational-ed center with my blessing. He does so well that he'll soon be a dealership intern. I could tell him to wait until he's been at the school a few more months, but timing and taking advantage of a budding passion should always trump the convenience of by-the-book teaching. Needless waiting only kills motivation. It's the same as continuing an intense class discussion past the period-ending bell: ideas in young people don't operate on schedule. This is why we don't have bells at West Valley. I just wait until a hot discussion ends, and then I say, "Now let's take a break."

I accommodate the students with special requests because my rules focus on each student, not the group or class. If the motivation is sincere and what they want to do is productive, I encourage them to follow their heart. In this way, West Valley is not only a model school for troubled students but also a model for solving troubles common to all teenagers, including scheduling conflicts.

In trying to make a difference with parents, I frequently call them at home or work to discuss their children's situations and to check on whether or not they're backing me up on the rules. Aside from calls and personal conferences, I also address parents once a month at our mandatory parent-night meetings. This typical agenda gives an idea of the range of topics I cover:

- Your child's health and exercise
- Punctuality and timeliness
- Talking back and talking to each other
- Profanity and saying things that you can't take back
- Neighborhood gang and crime issues
- Drugs, alcohol, and tobacco (yours, not theirs)
- Sexuality: growing up vs. being promiscuous
- Curfews (too tight . . . or too loose?)
- Jobs, working around the house, and developing a work ethic
- Calling the authorities: betraying your child . . . or saving his or her life?
- Your child's friends
- So if their life is falling apart, who's to blame?

On the parents' night when I discuss these items, the one that seems to draw the most interest is "Drugs, alcohol, and tobacco (yours, not theirs)." What has the parents squirming the most, perhaps because some of their children are present at the meeting, is the topic "Sexuality: growing up vs. being promiscuous."

On that night I also announce that for the first time I have taken the class to observe a local daytime Alcoholics Anonymous meeting. I'm always looking for new ways to attack common problems, and since many of my students come to West Valley with serious drinking habits or with parents with alcohol problems, a trip to AA makes practical sense. From what I can gauge afterward, the visit leaves a strong impression. Testimonials are given directly and touchingly to my students, connecting with them throughout the session. I tell the parents that I will make such visits regular events, rotating AA most likely with Narcotics Anonymous and Al-Anon/Alateen meetings.

I constantly tell parents and their children that having good character and a purpose in life must infuse everything that goes on at school and at home. In fact, as our academic-success pyramid reminds us, integrity and moral courage—along with hard work—precede academic achievement. These virtues are the foundation of learning; success on tests and in life are merely the effects, or result, of behaving honorably, of knowing right from wrong and living accordingly. As Ralph Waldo Emerson put it so eloquently, "The purpose of life is not to be happy. It is to be useful, to be honorable, to be compassionate, to have it make some difference that you have lived and lived well."

DREAMS THAT COME TRUE

Occasionally, my students have made an especially sweet difference in my own life. One such time was when a friend and I brought a busload of them to a campground by a beach in central California. They did all the things teenagers and two supervisory adults would do on such an overnight trip: goofing in the surf, walking on the beach, eating hotdogs and canned beans, roasting marshmallows over a log fire, gazing at the infinite number of stars in the night sky, and of course listening for raccoons and a rumored mountain lion.

After we cleaned up the eating area, some of the kids hiked up a slope among the pine trees to the restrooms and showers. Eventually, we sat around the fireplace telling stories and taking stabs at impersonating people.

Later, just before I headed for my tent, eight kids informed me that they wanted to stay up with their flashlights to play a teenage combination of tag and hide-and-seek. "Fine," I said. "Just keep your voices down and stay away from the occupied campsites. See you in the morning."

"Good night, Mr. White," Amy said, and the others chimed in.

"Good night, guys. And don't forget to put the fire out."

"I'll throw some water on it," another said.

"Perfect."

They sauntered off into the dark, following their little flashlight beams. With a shiver from the chill, I lifted my tent flap and squirmed into my sleeping bag. For a long while before I drifted into sleep I could hear their muffled voices. Ever so politely they had asked me permission to play a game. They played their game, and then I could hear them closer, gathered around the glowing embers of the fire. They were talking about their relationships, and then they took turns softly singing. I felt privileged to be with them. It didn't matter what they had been before they came to West Valley—addicts, gang members, criminals, dropouts, all of them rejects of one kind or another. I never saw them that way. What I saw was the good in them. I saw the normal kids they were at the campsite, the same boys and girls I see every day in their sweats and sneakers, poised to break through to the other side.

As I fell asleep, I never worried that they'd get into mischief or trouble during the night. With the rules in place, I trusted them. I was at peace as I slowly drifted off. Listening to some awkward crooning, followed by laughter, I felt like the luckiest teacher in the world.

For the record, the students whose stories I've highlighted in the book are a big part of my dreams come true. They've given me updates on their progress and current status.

Nola works part-time, attends college full-time, and studies for a bachelor's degree and a registered-nurse license.

Peter has one child and works in construction.

Kevin operates a hair salon, sells his own artwork, and is raising a son.

Marla, a fast-food worker, is set to graduate from high school.

Frankie is a fast-food worker.

Chris, in the Navy Reserve, is working toward his associate's degree, plans to join the U.S. Border Patrol, and is a licensed bail bondsman and bounty hunter.

Carlos, married, has moved back to California, works full-time, and attends college.

Rhonda runs a small boutique business in a shopping mall.

Alex is a married father of four and a highly successful high school teacher and baseball coach.

ULTIMATE MISSION

We need to build an education system whose ultimate mission is to help young men and women develop the moral courage, integrity, work ethic, and academic skills needed to become contributing, compassionate, law-abiding members of society.

My parents, both loving but firm teachers, long ago guided themselves by these precepts, precepts that worked then and still work for me now. They're also working well for a number of other teachers and administrators—some of them my former students, colleagues, even bosses. With a bit of new vision and a lot of heart, these colleagues are taking up the challenge and successfully imposing strong rules in other schools.

After my student Mark died in my arms, I had an epiphany and toughened my rules. I hope other educators don't have to go through such an ordeal, though most likely they've all "lost" students in one way or another. This alone should alert them that these losses are the consequence of not enforcing some moral code in schools. Most education leaders remember why they got into the profession: they wanted to save and shape the lives of children. Apart from the perennial struggles in education that have little or nothing to do with kids, I believe these men and women still know what's right and they know they're not doing it. Beneath their stuffy official façades, they still know that transforming the lives of children and not employing adults is what schools are really all about.

Schools

- To adopt some or all of my rules, you must be committed to enforcing them.
- Read your state's education code to find the legal support for what you are about to launch.
- By providing children with firm moral direction, you'll attack the cause of our failing schools and lost kids. The resulting effects will be obvious soon enough: gangs creep away, graffiti fades, respect for authority returns, bizarre or gang-related personal appearance and outfits disappear, a work ethic returns, racial harmony prevails, and test scores go up.

Parents

- Take the lead in insisting that schools reinstate the teaching of basic moral values as a foundation for academic achievement.
- Get together with other concerned parents and pull the fence sitters and naysayers onto your side.
- Meet with the school leadership and develop a workable plan to enforce the proposed rules.

EPILOGUE

They're waitin' for something that they feel is comin'.
Something important, and great.

—Thornton Wilder, *Our Town*

A growing number of Americans are also "waitin' for something . . . important, and great" to happen in the schools that teach our children and in the homes that raise them. Even as standardized test scores rise and reading and math levels increase, a disquieting voice within our collective national heart is telling us that the change we need to see must go deeper than this. We know intrinsically that our schools and homes need to spend less time teaching kids how to stay alive and a lot more time helping them understand what they're living for.

At West Valley Leadership Academy, we value improved reading ability not because it will look good on test results but because it enables our students to read to younger siblings, or to bring joy to someone who's lost his sight, or to motivate themselves with inspired tales of selflessness and courage, and to learn from them.

We celebrate our students' increased skill level in mathematics not because it will enable them to count all the money they'll make but because they'll be able to count the many ways they can use their money to help others.

I teach my students that the real purpose of learning history, science, economics, and government is not to memorize irrelevant factoids but to familiarize themselves with the timeless problems that have always confronted civilization so they can figure out how to try and solve them.

The stories you've read of my first twenty-five years with high-risk kids and, most recently, my experiences at West Valley Leadership Academy are not just the stories of poor urban children. They're really the stories of all our children, because violence, gangs, racism, drugs, alcohol, sexual promiscuity, and the disintegration of the family unit are moral issues that cross all racial, cultural, and socioeconomic boundaries. Sooner or later children everywhere will have to confront these challenges. They can surmount them and go on to lives of purpose, hope, and fulfillment if schools and parents apply the universal principles and rules I've shared in this book.

Americans need to stop waiting for this change to happen and start insisting on it, just as I did after my student died in my arms.

Parents

Stop waiting for better school leadership and start demanding that inept current leaders be replaced by morally courageous men and women who are not afraid to implement a values-driven system for teaching your children.

Schools

Stop waiting for parents to accept responsibility for their children's behavior and start demanding that they support the values discussed here at home and at school.

If this book has only entertained you with dramatic stories of one teacher and a handful of children, then its impact will be minimal and I've fallen short of my goal in writing it. I hope you're finishing these last pages not just with memories of someone's else's personal accomplishments but with a growing conviction that better teaching and parenting are possible for everyone. It's not about personality but about universal principles or rules that can be applied by anyone who's willing to commit to them. If you understand this, then you know everything you need to know to become a more effective teacher or parent, the kind who truly transforms children's lives and ultimately the world.